JUDGE NOT

JUDGE NOT

*A Selection of Sermons
preached in
Gray's Inn Chapel
1978-1988*

by

Eric James

Preacher to Gray's Inn
Chaplain to H.M. The Queen
Director of Christian Action
Fellow of King's College, London
Hon. Canon of St. Albans
M.A. (Cantab.) B.D. (Lond.)

Preface by
The Hon. Sir Gordon Slynn
Treasurer of Gray's Inn
and a Judge of the Court of Justice of the European Communities
and the Rt. Hon. Sir George Waller OBE
Dean of the Chapel, Gray's Inn, formerly a Lord Justice of Appeal

Christian Action

British Library Cataloguing in Publication Data

James, Eric, *1925-*
  Judge not.
  1. Church of England. Sermons
  I. Title
  252'.03

  ISBN 0-901500-37-2
  ISBN 0-901500-38-0 pbk

All profits from this volume will be given to the charity Christian Action

Published by:
Christian Action
St. Peter's House,
308 Kennington Lane,
LONDON SE11 5HY

First published 1989
© Eric James 1989

Printed by:
Russell Press, Bertrand Russell House, Gamble Street, Forest Road West,
Nottingham NG7 4ET

CONTENTS

Acknowledgements

To the Executors of the Estate of C. Day Lewis, The Hogarth Press and Jonathan Cape Ltd., for permission to include C. Day Lewis' poem 'Walking Away' from *The Gate* (1962);
to Faber and Faber Ltd., for permission to quote from *Markings* by Dag Hammarskjöld, translated by W.H. Auden and Leif Sjoberg; 'The Transfiguration' from *The Collected Poems of Edwin Muir* and from *For The Time Being* by W.H. Auden;
to the Executors and Trustees of the Estate of C.H. Dodd and Hodder & Stoughton Ltd for permission to quote from *The Johannine Epistles* by C.H. Dodd;
to SPCK for permission to quote from *Midrash and Lection in Matthew* by M.D. Goulder (1974);
to Macmillan Publishing Company for permission to quote from *Consequences; Truth and . . . .* by Daniel Berrigan, SJ (1967)

FOREWORD

It was well over twenty years ago that I preached at Evensong at St. Paul's Cathedral for the then Dean, Walter Matthews. Afterwards, he asked me back to the Deanery for supper, then a huge and distinguished house to the south of St. Paul's, which had lost most of its windows in the Second World War. Dean Matthews was a lonely widower, and the house that evening was shrouded in gloom. The portraits of famous deans who looked down upon us in the entrance hall were like ghosts of the past. At the supper table, I felt the need to bring some joy to the evening, and, as a conversational gambit, I asked the Dean what occasions in his ministry had most brought him happiness. Suddenly his eyes lit up and a smile spread over his face. "It gave me a delicious and mischievous joy one day, when I was Preacher to Gray's Inn" he said "to lean over the pulpit and say slowly to the judges and barristers before me the two words: 'Judge Not'." Silently he savoured his memory of the occasion for a few moments, and then added: "They all looked as though I had put them out of a job!" After that reminiscence, many another followed. We had a memorably happy evening.

Little did I know that in due course I would be privileged to be one of Walter Matthews' successors as Preacher to Gray's Inn and that his memory that evening would provide me with the title of this book of sermons and addresses.

Addresses to judges and barristers — even though they are joined by their wives, husbands, families and friends and young students, when they hear them — might seem at first sight simply the concern of those whose profession is the Law. But those who have the exacting responsibility of judging do so on our behalf, not instead of us. These addresses, therefore, although delivered first to no "ordinary" congregation — how could it be, when the Chapel is technically called a "peculiar"? — were prepared for people who are eager to receive an intelligent presentation of the Christian faith clearly related to

1

their particular needs and contemporary concerns. The Chapel of Gray's Inn is not only "open to the public" but warmly welcomes all who want to come to it; some, indeed, of the congregation regularly travel fifty miles, after a busy week, to be present in Chapel on a Sunday.

It needs also to be underlined that judges and barristers, like Shakespeare's Richard II, "live with bread, feel want, taste grief, need friends". They would be the first to repudiate any suggestion that they are not, in any fundamental sense, "ordinary people". Some of the most certain facts of their lives, as of all of us, are suffering and death. So these addresses not only relate the Gospel to Judgment in Court. They were delivered to people who, over a decade now, I have come to regard as much my friends as, for instance, the congregation of St. Stephen's, Rochester Row, Westminster, where I was a curate in the 50's; or the students to whom I once ministered in Trinity College, Cambridge; or the inner city congregation of St. George's, Camberwell in South London, the parish where I was once vicar; or the congregation of the cathedrals of Southwark and St. Albans where I have served as a Canon. In the Chapel, I marry some of the members of Gray's Inn — and their sons and daughters; baptise their children and grandchildren; and, alas, all too frequently, conduct the funeral or memorial service for one of their number.

It would, nevertheless, be true to say that, after ten years, I find the members of the Inn less intimidating than I did on my first Sunday as their Preacher in 1978. (To be "up before" a Bench of barristers as Preacher can be very forbidding to someone relatively ignorant of the Law!) I have now a far greater understanding and sympathy for those who, week in, week out, have the heavy responsibility of "truly and indifferently" ministering justice. I count it a privilege to be priest and pastor to the congregation of Gray's Inn — as well as Preacher (for no preacher can preach unless he is also priest and pastor) — especially at such a time as this, when a Christian interpretation and understanding of Law, Order and Justice in our society is so crucial.

Sermons are delivered at Gray's Inn only on three Sundays of each of the legal terms, so some of the major feasts of the Church are therefore "out of term"; but the great and central truths of the Christian faith are relevant "seven whole days, not one in seven" and are "in season, out of season". It will be observed that several of these sermons were, in fact, preached on Remembrance Day, which some clergy nowadays find frankly a difficult day on which to preach the Gospel. For myself, I know of no day on which the Gospel of our creation, preservation, and of the redemption of the world by our Lord Jesus Christ, has more to say.

A preacher is inevitably a plagiarist — at least, *I* am! ("Plagiarists" said Disraeli "at least have the merit of preservation".) It's not that I consciously *steal* 'other men's flowers' — that would never do in the Chapel of an Inn of Court! — but more a case of "What hast thou which thou hast not received?" And I'm not very good at recording who said — or wrote — what, and where. I know, for instance, that I owe much of the sermon on *Baptism and Piero della Francesca* to my good friend Timothy Schroder, Curator of Decorative Arts at the Los Angeles County Museum of Arts, and much of *Kipling and Remembrance* to the Revd. Charles Gordon Clark; but I hope that all who recognise the pearls they cast before me will be forgiving.

I should like to thank most sincerely the Treasurer and Masters of the Bench of Gray's Inn for first suggesting that this selection of the sermons preached to them should be published and then for generously helping to make publication a practical possibility. I am also grateful to the present Treasurer and the Dean of Chapel who have added kindness to kindness by contributing a Preface. ("Woe unto you when all men shall speak well of you! for so did their fathers to the false prophets"!) I must also thank the Council of *Christian Action* who have greatly helped, not least by encouraging Mrs. Jane Spurr, their secretary and mine, to type my manuscript, which she has done with her characteristic care and skill.

Eric James
Kennington
December 1988

PREFACE

Canon Eric James was invited to take up the ancient office of Preacher to Gray's Inn in 1978, in part, but only in part, because of the high reputation he had established as Chaplain of Trinity College Cambridge.

During the years which followed he has preached sermons on Sundays during the dining terms of the Inn to congregations largely, but not exclusively, composed of Members of the Inn — judges, barristers and students — and their families and friends.

They were the sort of sermons which people wanted to read again and to keep. At our suggestion copies were made available to those who wanted them; again at our suggestion this selection is to be published, so as to be available not just for us but for a wider group of readers.

Some of the sermons reflect the fact that he was preaching to lawyers; but the range is considerable and the sermons record many of the events and the moral and political issues of the last ten years — the Falklands, Enniskillen, AIDS, the trial of Steve Biko. Prepared to be spoken, they are yet the stuff that literature is made of, though many familiar with his voice on the radio will, at the same time, readily hear the intonation and the emphasis which he gave when speaking.

The style is direct, the expression elegant, sometimes startling and by no means conventional "sermonese". Just as the quotations and the humour assured total attention to every spoken word, the written text makes attractive, often compelling, reading.

Some of the views expressed may to some of his hearers have been no less startling; it should not be assumed that every member of his congregation agreed with everything he said. But everyone present would agree that Sunday by Sunday they were provoked to think, to question, often moved to an awareness of, and compassion for, the intense difficulties which individuals can face in our contemporary world. Reading the sermons makes one conscious of what motivates Eric James the priest in his total dedication to the pastoral side of his work, for which many of our Members and even more outside, have profound reason to be grateful.

We at Gray's Inn take great pleasure that these sermons are now in permanent form; we have no doubt that they will give interest, comfort and delight to many.

Gordon Slynn
Treasurer of Gray's Inn.

George S. Waller
Dean of Chapel.
23rd December, 1988

A FIRST SERMON

Gray's Inn Chapel: April 9th 1978

"What will this babbler say?" . . . "And he preached unto them Jesus and the Resurrection."

Acts 17 v.18.

Anyone who is appointed Preacher to this Ancient and Honourable Society can be sure that you will evince some interest in what the man you have appointed has to say — at least on his *first* Sunday! Perhaps, in view of your particular profession, you will not use the sort of words those Epicureans and Stoics of Athens used of St. Paul. But from the kindness of your dealings with me in these last weeks, I feel confident of your interest — and, indeed, of your warm concern — for what your new Preacher will have to say — *and be*; and I am very grateful for that, even if I am somewhat apprehensive.

And there is no doubt in my mind as to what the subject of my preaching to you should be this Second Sunday after Easter. I must follow the example of St. Paul, and preach to you "Jesus and the Resurrection."

But how? — on this first Sunday of my ministry among you, when one of the chief equipments of a preacher — his knowledge of his hearers' needs — is as yet inevitably small.

I have found that when I have little personal knowledge of those to whom I am called to preach, there is one infallible rule: to preach to oneself: to speak to one's own needs — in the hope that applying the ointment of the Gospel to my own wounds, so to speak, I may in some way the more recommend that salve to others — and to preach on one of the fundamental aspects of nature and of human need which "makes the whole world kin".

It so happens that each Easter of the last years has had for me a curious habit of being the occasion of some new experience of

7

bereavement; and this year has been no exception. In the last ten days I have assisted at the burial of a young and much loved doctor, and also of a close friend of mine, a fellow priest, who spoke to me on the telephone late on Good Friday night, complaining of exhaustion, and who was probably dead within an hour or so of that 'phone call.

"What will this babbler say?" Today I must speak — to myself at least — of "Jesus and the Resurrection".

On Easter Sunday two years ago I was preaching in the lovely priory church of St. Margaret, King's Lynn. The last time I had preached there was five years before, at the memorial service to a young priest, Tom Wood, who died of leukaemia, at the age of thirty-three. That Easter Saturday evening I sat in the church asking again what had Easter to say about the death of a young person like that? (I might as well admit to you this morning that I have to work through slowly, again and again, what I believe, and why: belief rarely comes easily to me in a nice neat creed — not even belief about "Jesus and the Resurrection".) That evening, as I sat there in the darkened church, I found myself asking again: who allowed Tom Wood to happen, so to speak? — a marvellously loving person, full of zest for life, full of fun. Who allowed his gifts of friendship, his gifts as a father, and husband, and priest? — gifts, many of which had been evoked not least by your last Preacher, Sydney Evans. Who allowed the bravery that some of us were privileged to watch at close quarters in St. Bartholomew's Hospital in those last months of his life? — the courage in his sweating away there, and the jokes, and the prayers: prayers that were sometimes half expletives. Who allowed the pastor that was Tom to "happen"? — the pastor to patients, and doctors, and nurses. And who allowed the skill of his doctors and nurses?

As I sat there, questioning within myself, some sort of answer formed to my questions. So next morning, Easter morning, in a church bedecked with daffodils, and flooded with sunlight, I preached a sermon on the text "the stone, huge as it was, had been rolled away already" — for that is what it felt like to me.

After a good lunch, I got in the train at King's Lynn to get back to my home in St. Albans. I'd not been home long when the 'phone rang. "I'm sorry to have to break the news to you" said a friend of mine "but I thought you'd want to know; Thomas Igloi was found dead in bed on Easter Saturday. He'd had a massive heart attack." Thomas was a person from whom some of you will in fact have received, indirectly. He was Professor of the 'Cello at the Royal Academy of Music — a Hungarian refugee; not yet thirty years old; a pupil of Casals, he had made his début at the Proms only a year before; he was the teacher of Anup Biswas, a young Indian friend of mine who played to you last year in Hall one Friday after dinner. Thomas Igloi and I had become close friends as together we tried to look after Anup.

Thomas Wood; Thomas Igloi. It seemed incredible that yet another Thomas should have been ripped away from this world in the prime of his life — and at such a time. I was angry with God for quite a few days: what I suppose the pundits would nowadays call "bereavement anger". Before I set out for Thomas Igloi's funeral that Easter Week I thought about him much as I had thought about my other good friend, Tom. Who allowed Tom Igloi to happen? Where did those marvellous gifts of music-making come from: his wonderful gifts of interpretation? Who gave him the gift of friendship which already made him so loved by his pupils? I could not believe it was all blind chance, accident, the result only of chaos — though his death had all the elements of an anarchic chaotic act about it. Joy did not in fact return to me for several days. But the stone — huge as it was — as I thought of Thomas, with a marvellous recording by him of a Schubert Quintet to help me — the stone, so to speak, began to be rolled away.

I could only believe that Tom was the product of the creative love of God that had issued forth in Jesus Himself: in his life, and love, and suffering. I could only believe that the love revealed on the Cross held some explanation of Tom's death as well as Tom's life. I could only believe that one day what now I saw only "in a glass, darkly", as "puzzling reflections, enigmas, in a mirror," I would see clearly as nothing but the action of the Creative Suffering Almighty Love of God.

When Tom Wood lay dying in St. Bartholomew's Hospital, he had copied out for me some writings from the great French spiritual writer of the 18th century, Jean Pierre de Caussade: thoughts which he said had literally "kept him going" in hospital. Let me read them to you this Second Sunday after Easter:-

> The life of faith is nothing but the continual pursuit of God through everything that disguises, disfigures, destroys, and, so to say, annihilates him.
> God teaches the heart not primarily by ideas but by pains and contradictions.
> Our understanding wishes to take the first place among the divine methods: it must be reduced to the last.
> All we have to do is to receive what we are given — and allow ourselves to be acted upon.

The story of "Jesus and the Resurrection" is not about Someone who was the Light that failed, and who was then switched on again:

9

about a man who gave up the ghost, and was then miraculously rescued on Resurrection Day. It's about a Man who received all that he was given by his loving Father as though it was a gift. He "allowed himself to be acted upon", so that instead of simply being the victim of his circumstances, by the way he approached the things that happened to him, he became the Victor. Resurrection Life in him *before* he died enabled him to suffer triumphantly. He wasn't miraculously released from the Cross. He was able to say because of what the Life that was in him enabled him to be and do: "It is finished" — accomplished, achieved, complete.

When *we* die, we are not able to take those words on our lips. There is always at our deaths much that is left incomplete: papers still to be attended to on our desks, and much that needs to be forgiven. Yet we too in our lives now can reveal, this side of the grave, as Jesus did, what I will call "Resurrection Life": in our work, our leisure, our home life and our friendships, our active life and our sufferings, not least in our bereavement. As the time comes for us to say on this earth farewell to our friends, one by one — as I have had to say farewell in these last few days to John Francis Thackeray Allison and to Derek Morris Phipps Tasker — we can commend those we love to him whose love and power was revealed not only in Jesus himself but in their own lives. And, please God, we ourselves will be able to make more and more our own the words of the 17th Century Puritan Divine, Richard Baxter:

> Lord, it belongs not to my care
> Whether I die or live;
> To love and serve thee is my share,
> And this thy grace must give.

> Christ leads me through no darker rooms
> Than he went through before;
> He that unto God's Kingdom comes
> Must enter by this door.

> My knowledge of that life is small,
> The eye of faith is dim;
> But 'tis enough that Christ knows all,
> And I shall be with him.

"What will this babbler say?" . . . "He preached unto them Jesus and the Resurrection."

A STREETCAR NAMED DESIRE

Gray's Inn Chapel: July 9th 1978

"Between us and you there is a great gulf fixed".

Luke 16 v.26.

It was Tennessee Williams' play *A Streetcar Named Desire* which first provoked me to preach on this text, way back in 1952, when I was a curate in Westminster. *Streetcar* had been produced at the Aldwych Theatre in 1949, and I had gone to see it there, with Vivien Leigh in the leading role, when I was a student, across the road at King's College. I was enthralled by it. The film version came out in 1952. I went on my day off as a curate to see it. There were some astonishing differences between the play and the film, though the leading part in the film was again brilliantly played by Vivien Leigh — with Marlon Brando instead of Bonar Colleano. I hastened to see Claire Bloom in the West End revival of the play a couple of years ago. But it was a late night showing of the film recently — twenty-five years old — that made me resolve to preach again on this great text: "Between us and you there is a great gulf fixed".

The story of *Streetcar* concerns two sisters. Blanche is about five years older than Stella. Blanche, at the beginning of the film — and the play — is trying to find the apartments of her sister in a run-down area of New Orleans. This is her first visit to Stella's new home, and it's rather a shock when she finds it's such a slum. Blanche and Stella had been brought up in somewhat better circumstances: a prosperous plantation by the Mississippi. At the beginning of the play, Blanche stands, bewildered, looking up at the two-storey slum, divided into flats. She's rather daintily dressed in white: dressed really, for a cocktail party. She looks like a white moth.

11

Blanche wouldn't have made the long journey to stay with her sister if it hadn't been necessary. She has been thrown out of the school where she has been teaching, because of some suspected misdemeanour with one of the pupils. Later on, the truth comes out. Blanche has been living as a prostitute for some time. She had got married when she was almost a child. Soon after the marriage, her husband had walked out on her. As Blanche puts it: "Since then, I have always depended on the kindness of strangers".

Stella doesn't know, and doesn't suspect, anything of the kind. She is a genuine, kind-hearted girl, and very fond of Blanche. During Blanche's stay, Stella is always trying to put in a good word for her. Most of this defence is for the benefit of Stella's husband, Stanley. Stanley is a man of rough humour; of almost animal joy. He is hearty with all men; loves his drink and his game of poker. His rough masculinity is in all his movements and all his attitudes. He sizes up women at a glance, with fairly crude classifications. Again and again he is insulting and unfaithful to Stella; but she stays with him. She understands him, and she loves him. She can't help forgiving him, no matter what he does to her.

It doesn't take long for Stanley to see through all the paint and powder of Blanche; and in spite of what he knows about her, while his wife is in hospital having a baby, Stanley "interferes with" Blanche, with the result that she goes out of her mind and has to be forcibly removed to a mental hospital.

The last scene of the play is different from the last scene of the film. In the play, Stella once again forgives Stanley — or at least she gives in to him: surrenders herself to helpless crying and to Stanley.

In the film, Stella *cannot* forgive Stanley. At the end of that last scene, she descends the rickety outside stairs, taking the baby with her. Stanley, crying like a baby tears of penitence and love for Stella, yells from the top of the staircase to Stella: "Stella! Stella!" — yells for her to forgive him and come back. But this time he has gone too far. Between Stella and Stanley there is "a great gulf fixed".

The two different endings explain why I have told you at such length the story of *Streetcar*. To forgive or not to forgive: that is the question. And it's a very biblical question.

What a Mary Magdalene of a person Blanche is! You can't help wondering how Jesus would have judged her, dealt with her. He could have said: "Father, forgive her — she was married so young, betrayed; she didn't really know what she was doing". And Stanley — the animal, the lovable animal, Stanley — born in a slum; quickly penitent; generous hearted; passionately loving as well as passionately lusting. What would Jesus say of him? Would He have told Stella to go back to him once again, in spite of all he had done?

— To forgive this seventieth times seven? Or would He have said: "No. Sometimes the great gulf must be fixed".

This very complex question — "To forgive or not to forgive" — seems almost to be part of the stuff of life here on earth: giving yet another chance — another "last chance" — to the young offender; the priest hearing the same old sin confessed with pathetic regularity; the parent hoping against hope that the returned prodigal will not go off again; but he does — and comes back, yet again.

Recently I've seen someone I've not seen for six years because he was so unrepentantly unjust to someone else: I simply have not known how to handle the forgiveness question. Nor have any whose advice I have asked.

Stella, Blanche, Stanley — all of us — are in some degree involved in this confusing business of forgiving people and being forgiven: of judging people and being judged. To fix the great gulf or not to fix it? That is the question.

And so we come to the passage from the Bible which has provoked my sermon. It's another of these stories of forgiveness and judgment — but a story with a difference. It's the story of Dives and Lazarus. Dives, the rich man, and Lazarus, the poor man, both die — so this is a story of forgiveness and judgment in the next life. The rich man is in torment, and now he is begging the beggar to be sent to his aid. But beyond the grave, the great gulf is fixed — absolutely fixed. Now there is Someone who knows all the rights and wrongs. Now there is no possible injustice or miscarriage of justice. Now there is no uncertainty, no confusion. What was hidden — all the mixture of motives — has been revealed. And God, whose hatred of evil is matched by his mercy, has judged. The great gulf is fixed, once and for all.

Who knows? Perhaps before that Judgment Seat Blanche would be a kind of Lazarus; going into Heaven before the rest of us. Perhaps even Stanley would be found a place before you and me. Who knows? We don't know: God alone knows.

Then what *do* we know?

First, that God alone knows. That is literally true.

Second: God alone knows, and God alone loves: God alone perfectly loves. In Christ He not only ate with publicans and sinners; He gave his life for them.

Third: God alone truly hates evil: all that keeps us from being what He means us to be: all that stops a Blanche or a Stanley — or ourselves — from being all we're meant to be.

Fourth: God alone can make the imperfect perfect: can make a silk purse out of a sow's ear. He took even the crown of thorns and wove it into a crown of glory. He can take even a Blanche and turn her

13

into a Saint Mary Magdalene. But he doesn't do it on this earth without our help. And sometimes as part of love — His love — a gulf has to be fixed, even on this earth.

Fifth: in the end, God alone will judge — with absolute love and absolute justice — Dives, Lazarus, Blanche, Stanley: those who in their upbringing on earth are almost out of range of the voice of God, and us today who have heard the word of God: the word of His love, His judging love.

Finally; when God forgives, he doesn't just surrender to us — as perhaps Stella did to Stanley. He doesn't give us "cheap grace". All his grace is costly to Him. That, as I understand it, is one meaning of the Cross at the heart of our faith. And he who told the story of that "great gulf fixed" spent his life, his life-blood, bridging that very gulf.

THE MARVEL AND MYSTERY OF MEMORY

Gray's Inn Chapel: November 12th, 1978

"Remember Jesus Christ"

2 Timothy 2 v.8.

November is the month of memory. It begins with the remembrance of All Saints and of All Souls. Then comes the Fifth:

Please to remember
The Fifth of November
    Gunpowder treason and plot;
We know of no reason
Why gunpowder treason
    Should ever be forgot

Then, at Remembrance-tide, our November memories enfold those who might have been the light and lamp of their times but for the savagery and slaughter of war.

November is the month of memory. Yet, really, it's very difficult to say what memory is. We talk of having a "good memory"; so that we can recall particular events in war, and particular people, whom perhaps we shall never now see again — in this world. But it really is very difficult to say what memory is. It's nothing like a toe or a tooth that can be touched. It's more an activity than an object; or, rather, it's a vast number of complex inter-related activities and processes. And I want to invite you first of all simply to be thankful for the marvel and mystery of those processes of memory, without which it would be impossible for us to confront and understand life

15

itself. Let us be thankful for our basic memory processes: learning, recalling, retaining, forgetting.

Wonder is the gateway to worship: wonder at the marvel of our gifts, our most everyday and common gifts; and I believe we need particularly to wonder at the gift of memory.

Supposing, for instance, I read you some poetry — perhaps from a Great War poem of Wilfred Owen:

> What passing-bells for these who die as cattle?
> Only the monstrous anger of the guns.
> Only the stuttering rifles' rapid rattle
> Can patter out their hasty orisons.
>
> No mockeries for them from prayers or bells,
> Nor any voice of mourning save the choirs, —
> The shrill, demented choirs of wailing shells;
> And bugles calling for them from sad shires.

I've read that poem a hundred times and more, and heard it sung in Britten's *War Requiem*, but I don't yet know it off by heart. It's not easy to remember. We could all learn it if we concentrated — perhaps some quicker than others, and some slower. But a little thought at just what happens when we memorise such a verse can cause in us a 'rebirth of wonder': thankfulness, born of wonder, for this marvel and mystery of memory, about which we know, as yet, so very little. We know that microscopic bio-chemical action is involved in every memory. But think of what goes on when we decide *not* to remember: when we decide to remember that particular verse: to select for memory that particular verse and not another. The way we can select what to remember is a marvel. The way, with our capacity to remember all that is happening around us and to us, we can eliminate all but a small and special selection, so as not to be overwhelmed and confused by a mass of memories: that surely is a marvel.

Yet almost as soon as I talk of the wonder of memory, I find myself wanting to talk about suffering; for all sorts of phrases come into my mind like "loss of memory". One thinks of those who suffered shell-shock in the Great War — and "failing memory", now that the Armistice of the Great War is so long ago. And it is the aged, most of all, who say from their experience: "We will remember them".

We all have memories so painful that sometimes we wish they could be forgotten or erased. I still remember as a boy the smoking rubble of houses round the corner from my home, with people with tin helmets working under the glare of arc lights, searching in the rubble for one of my fellow choir-boys who had been killed by a land-mine dropped that night.

The marvel of memory introduces us to so much pain.

Sarah Churchill, in her book *A Thread in the Tapestry*, begins her portrait of her father with sentences written in those last sad years of Churchill's life in which she and other members of the family were made to remember that, in spite of the accolades and honours that were heaped upon him, there was at the heart of his being a void which no achievement or honour could ever fill.

"On one of his birthdays" she writes "in answer to my sister Diana's exclamation of wonderment at all the things he had done in his life, he said: 'I have achieved a great deal to achieve nothing in the end.' We were listening to the radio, and reading the always generous newspaper eulogies. 'How can you say that?' she said. He was silent. 'There are your books' I said. 'And your paintings' Diana followed. 'Oh yes, yes, there are those.' 'And, after all, there's us' we continued. 'Poor comfort we know at times; and there are other children who are grateful to you that they are alive.' He acknowledged us only with a sad smile."

When there has been an early failure in the relationship between a child and his parents, as there had been in Churchill's case, we know now that an intense vulnerability is the result. Henceforth the perspective of memory is altered, and often what is recalled is in dark and sombre colours.

Anthony Storr, the psychiatrist, has written: "In the ordinary course of events, we know, a child takes in love with his mother's milk. A child who is wanted, loved, played with, cuddled, will incorporate within himself a lively sense of his own value; and will thereby surmount the inevitable set-backs and disappointments of childhood with no more than temporary sorrow, secure in the belief that the world is a predominantly happy place and that he has a favoured place in it. And this pattern will generally persist throughout his life. A child, on the other hand, who is unwanted, rejected or disapproved of, will gain no such conviction. Although such a child may experience periods of success and happiness, these will neither convince him that he is lovable, nor finally prove to him that life is worthwhile. A whole career may be dedicated to the pursuit of power, the conquest of women, or the gaining of wealth, only in the end to leave the person face to face with despair and a sense of futility, since he has never incorporated within himself a sense of his value as a person, and no amount of external success can ultimately compensate him for this — can rid him of the memory of his early experience of rejection."

Churchill certainly reveals all that. But he also reveals that memory is not all sad and sour. How many of his writings depended on the pleasures of memory — of his memories:

My African Journey;
My Early Life;
Great Contemporaries.

Churchill read voraciously, and he remembered what he read. Violet Bonham Carter wrote that "he read, as the hungry eat, neither from habit nor from duty, but from need. His books entered his system and became a part of him. He thought with his heart and felt with his mind." She tells us how she would approach Churchill through his memory. "The right way to his mind was through his heart and his imagination" she wrote. "I have spent hours with him in fruitless argument, battering in vain on a closed door. But if by some lucky phrase, some form of words, some vivid image, I could find the way to his imagination or emotions all barriers would fall. His intellect was often a closed book, but his heart was an open city."

There is no need for me to remind you why I take the memory of Churchill for my example. He had the great gifts of memory: learning, recalling, retaining, forgetting; and they brought with them the kind of courage which enables us to stand unflinchingly in the face of danger; the courage which can even shine brightly when there is little of it about. But it was only at certain times in his career that his gifts of memory exemplified the power of memory to confront suffering. At other times, great as Churchill was, he was the very epitome of the suffering that memory brings.

You may now be wanting to say to me: "You have remembered Churchill, but haven't you forgotten your text?" No. I haven't — and I hope you haven't: with our marvellous processes of memory let us now recall it: "Remember Jesus Christ".

I have wanted to set our remembrance of Jesus within the setting of our other November memories, for it is not divided from them. Indeed, it is those very memories that evoke from us our need to "remember Jesus Christ".

If with our memories we can recall the example of a Churchill, how much more do we need to remember and reflect upon the example of Jesus, unique though it may be, and distinct from all other of our human remembrances: the example of His love and courage and triumphant suffering.

And when St. Paul tells us "Remember Jesus Christ", I am sure he would urge us particularly to do that when we are having to confront suffering, mental and physical: not least the suffering of bereavement; not least the suffering that our memories bring.

18

When I remember those who "laid down their lives for their friends", I find I need to remember Him who laid down his life to reveal the love of God for them and for us all: who died to bring about a change in us, not merely in those who were His contemporaries — Great Contemporaries and small, "One died for all" says St. Paul "that they which live should no longer live unto themselves but unto Him who for their sakes died and rose again".

It is surely the knowledge that we who have survived one — or two — World Wars are almost "back where we were" which adds the bitterness of dismay, self-reproach and even cynicism to the acute sense of personal and national loss that returns to us with our November memories; and it is this that may move us to "remember Jesus Christ". For we have all heard that He has power to effect a change in human lives, whether it be the life of a Francis in the Middle Ages or a Mother Teresa in contemporary Calcutta. We know what remembrance of Jesus can do; what commitment to Jesus can do: that remembrance of him for many has been part of a continuing and transforming friendship. And therein lies Hope.

I am glad today therefore to bid you be thankful for your memories and with your memories to be thankful for those who died in two world wars, and in Korea, Cyprus, Northern Ireland, and other places of battle.

I am glad to bid you be thankful for Winston Spencer Churchill and others of our born leaders, now dead.

But I would be failing you, and failing those who have died that we might live, did I not pre-eminently say to you today: if we want to know how to be triumphant in suffering; how to find some transcendent purpose to guide and motivate the whole of life; how to find a promise that will at least suggest how we may cope with our inevitable bereavements; how to find a sufficient reason for going on going on when thick darkness sometimes enshrouds our wounded psyches; how to come to peace with ourselves, and go on working towards peace between race and race and man and man — then, with those memories that are part of the best gifts of our humanity, we cannot do better than heed the words of St. Paul and

Remember Jesus Christ
risen from the dead

THE JOURNEY OF THE MAGI

Gray's Inn Chapel: January 21st, 1979

"A cold coming we had of it,
Just the worst time of the year
For a journey,
And such a long journey.
The ways deep and the weather sharp,
The very dead of winter".

If I were to ask you which member of Gray's Inn wrote those most apposite Epiphany lines, I'm sure most of you would say: "Ah, 'The Journey of the Magi' — T.S. Eliot". And you'd be quite right. But T.S. Eliot — like some preachers I know! — wasn't above lifting a good quotation when he saw one; and those particular lines he lifted, with hardly a word of amendment, from one of the greatest sermons in English literature, preached before the King's Majesty at Whitehall on Christmas Day 1622 by Bishop Lancelot Andrewes, whose commemorative window is on the north side of our Chapel.

I should like simply to read, first of all, a few paragraphs from that most marvellous sermon:

> It was no summer progress. A cold coming they had of it, at this time of the year, just the worst time of the year to take a journey, and specially a long journey in. The ways deep, the weather sharp, the days short, the sun farthest off, *in solstitio brumali*, the very dead of winter . . .
>
> And these difficulties they overcame, of a wearisome, irksome, troublesome, dangerous, unseasonable journey; and for all this, they came. And came it cheerfully and quickly, as appeareth by the speed they made. It was but *vidimus, venimus*, with them — they saw and they came; no sooner saw, but they set out presently. So as upon the first appearing of the star, as it might be last night, they knew it was Balaam's star; it

called them away; they made ready straight to begin their journey this morning. A sign they were highly conceited of His birth, believed some great matter of it, that they took all these pains, made all this haste, that they might be there to worship Him with all the possible speed they could. Sorry for nothing so much that they could not be there soon enough, with the very first, to do it even this day, the day of His birth . . .

And we, what should we have done? Sure these men of the East shall rise in judgment against the men of the West, that is us, and their faith against ours in this point. With them it was but *vidimus, venimus*; with us it would have been but *veniemus* at most. Our fashion is to see and see again before we stir a foot, specially if it be to the worship of Christ. Come such a journey at such a time? No; but fairly have put it off to the spring of the year, till the days longer, and the ways fairer, and the weather warmer, till better travelling to Christ. Our Epiphany would sure have fallen in Easter week at the soonest.

Great prose. Great preaching.

But it raises for me great problems.

I suppose the historicity of the journey of the Magi is as dubious as any event in the whole Gospel record. Epiphany stories are, of course, common in ancient writing about holy men. It is most often mythical material used to make a point: in this case, that Gentiles accepted the offer of salvation which Jews refused.

But, to that mythical material, Andrewes — with a preacher's desire to be real and relevant to his hearers — adds all the imagery of an English winter: cold, frost and snow, and the sun far off. And in endeavouring to make the story local and familiar, the fundamental question "Did it happen?" and if it did, "What's its significance?" gets lost.

The temptation is still with every preacher at Epiphany: to try and fulfil what he thinks are many people's expectations at such a time, and do a kind of Christmas-card-that's-arrived-a-bit-late sort of sermon: kings, camels, dew drops on the cradle — the lot; all the Christmas "kitch" beloved by hymnographers — and Marks and Sparks — and indeed Marshall & Snellgrove — and not only by them; all that stuff that hasn't an ounce of evidence in the Gospel record, but at Christmas and Epiphany goes down a treat.

But the message of the Gospel, to my mind, is too important for it to get lost in all that. It's curious, for instance, that in these weeks we've all been singing lustily about "Three Kings from Persian Lands Afar", but rarely have we stopped to ask: "What has the Gospel to do with one king from Persian lands afar — the Shah — and his people — and the lorry drivers' strike?"

Christmas and Epiphany can so easily be a "trip" — a drug trip on what Marx rightly called — though he was quoting Charles

21

Kingsley — "the opium of the people": religion. We go off on our romantic camels — looking like kings with our paper hats; but the journey doesn't end up bringing us closer to the revelation of who God is: not to a God who can help us to make sense of our real world.

I read this week the words of an African leader in newly independent Mozambique, bitterly critical of the nakedness of the Church before the Marx-inspired movements which he said seem to hold the key to the future not only of his own country, but of, he said, in due course, the future of the whole of southern Africa. "The Western Church has failed completely to prepare us for independence" he said, "both practically, in terms of a locally trained leadership, and theologically, in terms of being able to relate the Christian faith to the aims and achievements of our newly created socialist society."

I've been trying to think this week what I would say this Epiphany about the Myth of God Incarnate and the Truth of God Incarnate if I were in Mozambique today, or if I were one of the few Christians in Iran; or if I were in a "chapel meeting" — significantly so-called — of the Transport and General Workers Union here in England, or for that matter with the CBI. And the word I've come up with which might make some sense of the Epiphany and the Incarnation, is one well understood in many circles today. It's the word SOLIDARITY.

The Incarnation is not a theory. It's God's revelation of his solidarity with us: God in such solidarity with us that he gives us an example that's bone of our bone and flesh of our flesh; and he gives us a call — and the grace and power to follow that call — to be in solidarity with our fellow human beings in their most pressing situations and their deepest human needs.

Theology is often these days called literally "God-talk" — Theos: God — Logos: Word — God: Word — God-Talk. But in this Chapel we read at the Carol Service the great Christmas Gospel that: "The Word was made Flesh". The Logos of the Theos had to be made *flesh* before people could understand it. They had literally to see his solidarity with them. The poor people, those who were being oppressed, had to see God's solidarity with them in Jesus. Theology was *done* in Jesus, not just talked; and now it has to be done wherever Christians — and not only Christians — meet: in initiatives in families, and between individuals, and in communities and localities, in national political action, in trades unions and managements; in action for justice, which is the first requirement of that love which God has revealed himself to be.

Let me illustrate what I've been trying to say with a story.

22

My predecessor, both as Chaplain of Trinity College Cambridge and as Vicar of St. George's Camberwell, the Trinity College Mission in South London, Geoffrey Beaumont, left Camberwell to become a monk. He joined the Community of the Resurrection; and they soon sent him off as a novice on something he hated: a Beach Mission on the sands at Felixstowe. He couldn't bear it; because people on holiday were "got at" by a preacher. And there were lots of callow students to help the preacher — or that was the theory!

Geoffrey had only to stand around in the crowd in his cassock — after he'd gathered the crowd for the preacher from their deck-chairs. He did, until he saw a notice: "Bathing Costumes for Hire". That did it. He slipped quietly away and hired one — 1950s model; black, with shoulder straps; got into it, and rejoined the crowd. A few minutes later, one of the students, not now recognising him without his cassock and his glasses, pursued him. "Have you been saved?" tenderly she enquired. "Saved?" he said "I haven't been *in* yet!"

There is a theological point to that story.

IN-CARNATION. Christmas and Epiphany are not *in the end* about candlelight, cribs, kings and incense in a sanctuary. They are about God in his world: inside the various situations which are most pressing. And we have to be immersed in those situations before we can work out what the Gospel has to say to them: what 'salvation' might mean.

It's curious, isn't it, that our Christmas carols and all the things that rightly so delight children at Christmas — and rightly delight the child in us — can, in fact, so easily turn our backs on the harsh realities of the world to which the Incarnation and the Epiphany are addressed. We are scared of the adult implications of Christmas: God's solidarity with us in the realities of his world, and his laying upon us the demand for us to be in solidarity with our fellow human beings. Yet the Myth of the Magi — in the profoundest sense of that word myth — is in the end about grown responsible men learning wisdom for their world from Jesus Christ our Lord: the Light of the World: The Light of *our* World.

THE TRIAL OF STEVE BIKO

Gray's Inn Chapel: February 4th 1979

What makes a great trial? Obviously, sometimes, it's the person on trial: Jesus, Thomas à Becket (to whom this chapel is dedicated), Joan of Arc. Clearly a trial can also be made great by a memorable judgment, or by a no less memorable (or notorious) judge or advocate. Then there's the subject matter: official secrets; a great train robbery; a particularly gruesome murder.

But let me alter this question a little. What makes a trial of great *religious* significance? Again, it could be the person on trial: Jesus, Becket, Joan of Arc, Thomas More, Bunyan. There's obvious and overt religious significance there.

But I want to suggest to you that the manner in which a trial is conducted is an implicit religious statement; for it makes clear what a nation thinks about justice, about freedom, about truth, about the value and significance of every individual.

These thoughts came to me this week because a book has recently been published called *I Write What I Like: A Selection of the Writings of Steve Biko*, who died on September 12th 1977, as a result of brain injury inflicted on him by one or more unidentified members of the South African police, while he was under detention in Port Elizabeth. The book is edited with a personal memoir by Fr. Aelred Stubbs of the Community of the Resurrection.

It was one of my tasks to get the book reviewed in the journal of *Christian Action*. I wrote to Sir Robert Birley, who was Headmaster of Eton for fourteen years, from 1949 to 1963; but who, on retirement, went from Eton, rather bravely and imaginatively, to be Visiting Professor of Education at the University of Witwatersrand, Johannesburg, from 1964 to 1967.

24

Sir Robert wrote in his review:

In recent months, a number of people have asked me if I thought that Steve Biko had been to some extent built up because of his horrifying end, and that if he had been reasonably treated he would not be regarded as especially important. Perhaps this was an inevitable reaction. So perhaps I had better make my own position clear. I first met Steve in August 1970, in Durban. Not long after, I was in London, and I was asked by a Member of Parliament, now a leading member of the Cabinet, who was going out to give a lecture in Durban, whom he ought to meet there. I said it might seem absurd, but I thought the most important person for him to see was an African medical student, as I felt sure that in thirty years time he would be Prime Minister of South Africa. The Member of Parliament took me seriously and had a long talk with the student. When he returned, he told me that he thought I was absolutely right — 'That young man *will* be Prime Minister of South Africa.'

But, for all that, looking forward to the years of turmoil that may well lie ahead, Steve Biko might well have become nothing but a name. That is why it is so important that this book has appeared. From his writings, and the wonderfully sympathetic picture of him given us by Fr. Aelred Stubbs, we can see what he was really like, and his personality will remain alive. This book will remain part of African history for generations to come.

It is also a book of the greatest importance for Englishmen today. Black Consciousness is a revolutionary movement, not in the sense that it will lead to changes brought about by violence, but that it is making millions of people think differently. It is giving the Africans of South Africa self-respect, by making them realise that they are going to make History. As Steve Biko put it to me once: 'We cannot come in under the umbrella of the White Liberals, because, if we do, the contribution we shall make to the future of the country will be a White one, and it must be a Black one.'

There is no doubt that the most difficult problem facing the supporters of Black Consciousness is that of their relations with White Liberals. In a sense, they feel that they must free themselves from the protection of their umbrella. Occasionally in consequence, they have been — or so it seems to me, an outsider from another country — unfair to them. There is one article in this book which has always made me feel uncomfortable, entitled *White Racism and Black Consciousness*. In order to escape from the White Umbrella, Steve Biko here has to belittle the efforts of the White Liberals in an exaggerated and unfair way. (It is significant that he uses about them the term "do-gooder". We should always be suspicious of a writer or speaker who uses it. I have no doubt that there were those who used it about the Good Samaritan.) But throughout the book there are passages which show a real appreciation of what some "Whites" are doing in South Africa. And perhaps I might add that, five minutes after Steve had made to me his remark about the "White Umbrella", he said, "Mind you, there's got to be a White contribution, too. We're not the

25

only people in this country!" And on personal relations between Black student leaders and White liberally minded student leaders, he said to me, "Personal relations — they're splendid! And on the basis of those personal relations we'll build the coalition".

A quarter of the book is taken up with the Personal Memoir of Steve Biko, written by Fr. Aelred Stubbs. It is of the utmost significance that it is written by a *White* man, and it is to be hoped that this will be appreciated two hundred years from now, when the book, I believe, will still be read. If I had to find one epithet for this Memoir it would be "understanding". It makes one understand Steve Biko, the quite remarkable strength of an utterly unflamboyant person, the richness of his personal relations, the originality of his mind. The title Fr. Aelred has given to his Memoir is significant: *Martyr of Hope.*

It was reading that remarkable review, and reading the book itself, with the personal memoir by a *monk*, from Eton, now living the Contemplative Life in Lesotho, which made me also read this week the book of the trial of Steve Biko — May 3-7 1976 — and of the inquest on his death, attended by Sir David Napley at the invitation of the Law Societies of South Africa, whose appraisal of the inquest is included in the book. The book *The Testimony of Steve Biko*, is written in part by the Dean of the University of Pennsylvania School of Law, and in part by the American lawyer who is Director of the Southern Africa Project of the Lawyers' Committee for Civil Rights Under Law, in Washington, Millard Arnold. Reading these books, and Sir Robert Birley's review, made it clear that because of the person on trial, Steve Biko's trial was a great trial. Perhaps I might also say that I found the inquest as memorable as the trial, not least because of the great distinction of the contribution of Counsel for the Biko family, Sidney Kentridge.

I also think that the person on trial makes the trial of Steve Biko of great religious significance. *Martyr of Hope* is not an extravagant title.

What is one to say of the manner of the trial, and the inquest, in a country which claims to be a Christian country and has a higher percentage of church-goers than almost any other society in the world? Let me quote just one sentence from Sir David Napley: "It is clear that an investigation conducted by experienced police officers with a little of the enthusiasm and vigour with which they customarily appear to question detainees would have elicited the truth from the security police in far less time than was necessary to demonstrate their mendacity in the witness box."

"Mendacity" is not a nice word; but it is obviously carefully chosen by Sir David, and it relates not only to the security police.

You may ask: But why do you preach to us about this?

Because it is just possible you may not always be conscious what a profoundly religious profession is yours: concern for justice, freedom, truth, and the value and significance of every individual: it is that, at least in part, which makes yours such a religious profession.

Again: because it is not impossible that some of you may have individual opportunities, and indeed, this Ancient and Honourable Society may have ways and means of sustaining those in other countries, like Sidney Kentridge, who as fellow members of your profession are doing what they can to prevent the legal system in their country becoming a derision.

Again: because there is reason surely to give thanks in such a place as this that the verdict reached at Steve Biko's inquest is unlikely to have been reached here: nor would, thank God, a Steve Biko in our country be the twentieth person to die in the custody of the police in eighteen months.

And we may also surely pray and resolve, in such a place as this, that whatever needs to be done, to see that no one in our society shall suffer injustice by reason of their race or their colour, shall be done.

DAG HAMMARSKJÖLD

Gray's Inn Chapel: May 5th 1979

My Cambridge diary for June 5th 1958, when I was Chaplain of Trinity College, Cambridge, says: "Degree Lunch: Dag Hammarskjöld: 11.45. Sing Grace. Choir: one madrigal and National Anthem."

I can remember that it was a splendid summer's day; and where I sat at lunch in Hall; and the dons' wives decked out gloriously; and a couple of undergraduates in court dress, as pages to the Vice-Chancellor: silk stockings and buckled shoes; and that it was a wonderful meal. I just wish I could remember what Dag Hammarskjöld said at the lunch! But what with the food, the wine, and the heat of the day . . . !

Fortunately, what he said is in his published works. It was an address about the central problem of all human relationships, private and public: trust. He called it "The Walls of Distrust". Hammarskjöld paid us the compliment of assuming we could take a half-hour discourse after lunch, with long and involved quotations from the Jewish philosopher, Martin Buber.

But Hammarskjöld was a serious man; and he came to us that day as Secretary-General of the United Nations, with a burden of serious problems upon his shoulders: Korea, China, Indonesia, Kashmir, Palestine, Hungary, North Africa. "There are fires all around the horizon", he said, "and they are not fires announcing peace". A fortnight before that Degree lunch, the delicate and almost equal balance between Christians and Moslems in the Lebanon had been tipped towards a Moslem majority by the influx of Palestine refugees — and the Moslem birth rate. There were riots that year, as this year, in Beirut, and considerable loss of life.

What kind of a man was that burden-bearing man? And why do I want to talk about him today?

Dag Hammarskjöld was born on 29th July 1905, in Uppsala. His father was the Swedish Minister of Education, then Minister of Justice, then a very unpopular Prime Minister during the First World War. After his retirement from the Premiership he became Governor of Uppsala, residing in the splendour of the town's massive red-walled 16th century castle. There Dag spent his childhood and adolescence, and went to school and university.

Dag's father, who came from a long line of soldiers and government officers, was emotionally aloof and patriarchal. But it was from his father's side Dag said he inherited the belief that "no life is more satisfactory than one of selfless sacrificial service to your country and to humanity".

Agnes Hammarskjöld, Dag's mother, whose forbears were scholars and clergymen, was the opposite of Dag's father. She was warm, generous, and overflowing with goodwill. Her bond with Dag was particularly close; and he continued to live at home, and spent many of his evenings with her, until her death in 1940, when he was thirty-five. From his mother he said he inherited the belief that "all men are equal as children of God."

As a student in the Uppsala of the 1920's, Dag Hammarskjöld saw at close quarters the beginnings of the movement towards Christian Unity. Archbishop Nathan Söderblom, its inspired leader, lived just across the way from the Hammarskjöld's. Söderblom and Dag's father shared the burden of the ceremonial occasions of that great city, and the Archbishop's son, Jon Olof Söderblom, and Dag were classmates at school and university.

At University, Dag's religious development was anything but smooth and straightforward. The Uppsala school of philosophy was marked by a critical attitude to religion, and to the Christian faith in particular, and for years Hammarskjöld was tormented with religious doubts and difficulties. At University, we can say his faith was eroded. He became a rebel against traditional church doctrine, and relied tremendously for his aesthetic and emotional satisfaction on the delights of nature. He was a keen mountaineer, and the satisfaction that gave him never grew stale on him.

It became clear at University that he was a brilliant scholar, outstanding at languages, in touch with all the latest developments in art and literature: Hesse, Thomas Mann, Katherine Mansfield, Rabindranath Tagore; he was at home in them all.

But there were other influences in Dag's life.

Albert Schweitzer came to lecture in Uppsala at Söderblom's invitation and to give organ recitals to support his hospital in the Congo. We don't know when Hammarskjöld began studying Schweitzer's writings. We know they once met, in Switzerland, in

29

Hammarskjöld's later life. In a climbing expedition in 1948 Hammarskjöld was absorbed in Schweitzer's *The Quest of the Historical Jesus*; and his library contained half a dozen or so of Schweitzer's works.

Another great influence on him was the writings of the mystics of the Middle Ages: Eckhart, St. John of the Cross and St. Thomas à Kempis. *The Imitation of Christ* was found by Hammarskjöld's bedside, in his New York apartment, after his death. He had an edition in his pocket when he was killed.

It was in the months immediately prior to his visit to Cambridge that Hammarskjöld came upon the writings of Martin Buber. On April 10th 1958 he wrote to Buber in Jerusalem saying how strongly he had responded to some of his writings, and then discovered Buber was in fact in Princeton. He immediately invited him to visit him at the United Nations headquarters in New York, where they had two hours' concentrated conversation. Buber has written that "he who stood in the most exposed position of international responsibility" was concerned about the same things as "I who stand in the loneliness of a spiritual tower". Hammarskjöld told Buber he was scheduled to talk at Cambridge and asked his permission to quote him at length, and they arranged to meet again in September in Jerusalem. They also met there the next year, in 1959. When Hammarskjöld's life came to an end, he was in the middle of translating into Swedish Buber's *I and Thou*.

But the Bible was certainly as great an influence as any on Hammarskjöld, and especially the Psalms. The English Prayer Book version of the Psalms was his constant companion.

Hammarskjöld had taken his first degree in 1924, and in 1930 moved with his family to Stockholm, to pursue his studies in economics and to embark on what at first promised to be an academic career. After getting his doctorate in economics, he became Secretary of the Royal Commission on Unemployment; then Under-Secretary of the Ministry of Finance; then Chairman of the Swedish Bank. In 1947 he was the Swedish representative at the Marshall Plan negotiations for the post-war reconstruction of Europe, and in 1951 Vice-Minister of Foreign Affairs and a non-party member of the Swedish government.

You might say that here was a young man with everything going for him. But that was not how it appeared to Dag. He thought he'd reached literally a dead end. He'd got to almost the highest rung of the Swedish political ladder, and was beginning to know the international scene; but inside him life was a void: meaningless.

We know this because of an extraordinary event: an extraordinary piece of writing. What no one knew, what none of his family or most of his intimate colleagues or friends so much as suspected, was that for nearly four decades, from his student days until a few weeks before his death, he had been in the habit of recording his most intimate reflections: on life and destiny; on nature's grandeur and mystery; on the temptations and dilemmas of public office — all in the context of his life-long resolute search for utter integrity and a dependable faith.

It was not just a diary he had been keeping, more a succession of notes, never intended while he was alive for the eyes of anyone but the author. After his death, the reflections recorded over the years were discovered in his desk, in the United Nations' building in New York, with an undated letter to a Swedish friend:

> These entries provide the only true 'profile' that can be drawn. If you find them worth publishing, you have my permission to do so — a sort of 'White Paper' concerning my negotiations with myself — and with God.

Well, people did find them worth publishing: in a book called, in English, *Markings*, translated by W.H. Auden, of which half a million copies were sold in the first six months. In December 1956 Dag wrote his own account of the origin of *Markings* as one of the entries in *Markings* itself:

> These notes? — They were signposts you began to set up after you had reached a point where you needed them, a fixed point that was on no account to be lost sight of. And so they have remained. But your life has changed, and now you reckon with possible readers, even, perhaps, hope for them. Still, perhaps it may be of interest to somebody to learn about a path of which the traveller who was committed to it did not wish to speak while he was alive. Perhaps — but only if what you write has an honesty with no trace of vanity or self-regard.

Those phrases disclose the mood of the book: exacting, self-questioning in pursuit of utter integrity, discovered in total commitment to God.

When Hammarskjöld began to put down those "Markings", some time between 1925 and 1930, he was, as I've said, a student in his 20's. His very first entry has this paragraph in it:

I am being driven forward
Into an unknown land.
The pass grows steeper,
The air colder and sharper.
A wind from my unknown goal
Stirs the strings
Of expectation

Still the question:
Shall I ever get there?
There where life resounds,
A clear pure note
In the silence.

Those entries continue through the years of his unbroken rise to public office and fame. But they're certainly not an uninterrupted upward movement of the spirit. They're much more a series of ascending thrusts and sharp declines, plunging sometimes towards despairing desolation. Then comes an abrupt and wholly unexpected crisis, a turning point, a decisive influence on the whole of the rest of his life.

That turning point was between 1952 and 1953: just before he took on what his predecessor, Trygve Lie, had called the "most impossible job on earth", Secretary-General of the United Nations. And the record of this crisis, in his "Marking" for Whitsunday 1961, is, in a sense, the most significant record in his whole journal:

I don't know Who — or what — put the question, I don't know when it was put. I don't even remember answering. But at some moment I did answer Yes to Someone — or Something — and from that hour I was certain that existence is meaningful and that, therefore, my life, in self-surrender, had a goal . . . As I continued along the Way, I learned, step by step, word by word, that behind every sentence spoken by the hero of the Gospels, stands one man and one man's experience.

After that crisis, the mood of questioning, of uncertainty, of inner struggle, persisted. But you can detect in the journal the progressive dominance of a peace and serenity grounded in ever deepening dedication.

Thou who art over us,
Thou who are one of us,
Thou who *art* —
Also within us,
May all see Thee — in me also,
May I prepare the way for Thee,
May I thank Thee for all that shall fall to my lot,
May I also not forget the needs of others.
Keep me in Thy love
As Thou wouldest that all should be kept in mine.
May everything in this my being be directed to Thy glory.
And may I never despair.
For I am under Thy hand,
And in Thee in all power and goodness.

Give me a pure heart — that I may see Thee,
A humble heart — that I may hear Thee,
A heart of love — that I may serve Thee,
A heart of faith — that I may abide in Thee.

Because he developed the habit of placing specific dates over individual "Markings", by comparing these dates with major public events, his travel calendars, and his cherished anniversaries — like his birthday, for which he always tried to get home to Sweden — it's often possible to establish the very circumstances which occasioned many of the reflections.

When he was drafted without warning into the Secretary-Generalship he writes:

I am the vessel. The draft is God's. And God is the thirsty one.
He who has surrendered himself to it knows that the Way ends on the Cross — even when it is leading him through the jubilation of Gennesaret or the triumphal entry into Jerusalem.

When re-elected to be Secretary-General for another five years, he remarks:

For someone whose job so obviously mirrors man's extraordinary possibilities and responsibilities, there is no excuse if he loses his sense of having been called. So long as he keeps that, everything he can do has a meaning, nothing a "price".
Your responsibility is indeed terrifying. If you fail, it is God, thanks to your having betrayed Him, who will fail mankind. You fancy you can be responsible *to* God; can you carry the responsibility *for* God?

Perhaps the most exacting challenge to Hammarskjöld was also his last: his efforts to mediate in the Congo Civil War.

It was with that Congo conflict sharpening towards its final crisis that he wrote:

Give us
A pure heart
That we may see Thee,
A humble heart
That we may hear Thee;
A heart of love
That we may serve Thee,
A heart of faith
That we may live Thee
Thou
Whom I do not know
But Whose I am

Thou
Whom I do not comprehend
But Who has dedicated me
To my fate
Thou —

Two months later, his plane crashed in Central Africa, to which he had flown in a last desperate attempt to mediate; and Hammarskjöld's service to humanity, and his personal spiritual pilgrimage, were brought to an early and tragic end.

What is clear is that in spite of his being engaged in such a purposeful life, and being surrounded by people for so much of his life, and having a number of intimate and rewarding friendships, in the most diverse circles — Barbara Hepworth, for instance, was a close personal friend — Hammarskjöld lived with a gnawing inner loneliness. He refers to it directly in his very first entry in *Markings*:

Friendship needs no words — it is solitude
delivered from the anguish of loneliness.

He writes to a friend: "There is an incurable loneliness of the soul."

In the first entry after that day that he went to Cambridge and shook hands and talked with many of us, he wrote:

Didst thou give me this inescapable loneliness so that it would be easier for me to give Thee all?

Only three months before he died, he writes of:

The voice of loneliness
Screaming for love.

It's not unusual to find people of an intense nature, who have to suffer the continuous hammer-blows of merciless public responsibilities, experiencing a spiritual aloneness which brings them sometimes to the verge of breakdown. Hammarskjöld admitted he found relief in work as an anaesthetic against loneliness. He felt that for him, with his temperament, in his position, loneliness was inevitable, and part of his duty. But he did not merely bear his loneliness stoically; he resolved it at a far deeper level:

Thou who has created us free . . .
Thou who at this time art the one among us who suffereth the uttermost loneliness
Thou — who art also in me,
May I bear Thy burden, when my hour comes . . .

It's not difficult these days to write off psychologically a man of brilliant and sensitive intellect, burdened by continual threats to the world's peace; a bachelor, with an emotionally aloof but dominating father, and a warm and tender mother; a man who found conventional social life exhausting. It's not difficult to do a hatchet job on such a person, with, of course, a psychological hatchet. So the headlines have been sensational: "The Secret Life that No one knew Existed": *Readers Digest*. "Hammarskjöld the Schizophrenic"; and so on. But the facts are that Hammarskjöld was neither anti-social nor without friends. He "communicated" socially. The probability is that he was more aware than most people of the simple truth that we are all ultimately alone. There's a very profound "Marking" in which he writes:

> He is one of those who has had the wilderness for a pillow, and called a star his brother.
> Alone. But loneliness can be a communion.

My own conclusion is that Dag Hammarskjöld plumbed the depths of his own loneliness and found something beyond it.

He wrote one day:

> Compelled or chosen — in the end, the vista of future loneliness only allows a choice between two alternatives: either to despair in desolation or to stake so high on the "possibility" that one acquires the right to life in a communion beyond the individual.
> But doesn't choosing the second call for the kind of faith which moves mountains?

Yes. It does.

And the significance of Dag Hammarskjöld is that he found such a faith, and found it in the midst of those years packed with the problems and complexities of world affairs.

Thus he wrote with conviction:

> In our era, the road to holiness necessarily passes through the world of action.

But that doesn't mean that for him action was all-important.

He was a man who travelled hundreds of thousands of miles in the cause of peace: to China, to Suez, to Thailand, and finally to the Congo. He never found a home in any one church. But he wrote from his own experience:

> The longest journey
> Is the journey inwards.

CAPITAL PUNISHMENT

Gray's Inn Chapel: July 8th 1979

The job of night porter is not always rewarding: but I spent a most profitable summer vacation, thirty years ago, as night porter of Cumberland Lodge in Windsor Great Park, when Sir Walter Moberly was its Principal, and I was still a student. I had heard Sir Walter deliver the 1949 Scott Holland Lectures on *The Ethics of Punishment*. I have never forgotten them — or him who gave them. And I've no doubt at all what he had to say much influenced my thinking on Capital Punishment.

I have a good deal of hesitation about addressing you on such a subject; but I've felt that none of us can afford to fail to refresh our minds from time to time on that complex but crucial subject — and particularly at this time; and where better to refresh our minds on a subject on which the Christian conception of justice and mercy has surely a peculiar contribution than in our Chapel?

One of the benefits of a great book on Punishment such as Sir Walter's is to give perspective to one's judgment, not least historical perspective, and not least by bringing humour to bear upon a subject in which humour might otherwise seem misplaced.

Sir Walter reminds us that, in the year 1595, the City Court of Leyden sentenced a dog that had killed a man to be hanged, and to remain hanging on the gallows, to the deterring of all other dogs; and his goods, if any, to be forfeited.

By that quotation he skilfully raises the question not of whether such punishment is in principle legitimate, but as to why such punishment in practice so often fails to deter.

On the other hand, official opinion, even if not wholeheartedly abolitionist, has advocated it, as the years have gone by, more temperately, and assigned to it only a limited scope.

To the man in the street it has seemed beyond question that fear of death is always and everywhere the strongest deterrent. Imprisonment for life is to him a far weaker thing. And this conviction is to him so self-evident that it really requires no support, and if it is questioned he feels irritation of the kind we all feel when confronted with sophistry.

This raises some worrying questions of politics; for there are obviously votes to be had in appealing for the support of the man in the street in this cause. Yet I suppose the supreme example of a leader who, tongue in cheek, set out to gratify the passions of the people which he did not himself share is Pontius Pilate, whose name as a result has been a by-word for nearly 2,000 years, and who washed his hands in vain.

Most of you will know only too well that the death penalty does not deter a large proportion of potential murderers: the passionate, the intoxicated, the mentally subnormal. It is only a minority of murders which are planned, and in which the intending murderer calculates the consequences; and even amongst murderers of the calculating type it has to be admitted that the terrorist and the bank robber, who are inured to taking risks, are not deterred by the prospect of the death sentence. On the contrary, the spice of danger, and indeed the possibility of becoming a hero and a martyr, may even be to the terrorist a stimulus and an incentive: as that gallant widow of a terrorist outrage, Jane Ewart-Biggs, has recently pointed out.

In the middle of the 19th century, when executions were still public, a prison chaplain, the Revd. R.W. Roberts, interrogated 167 persons under sentence of death as to whether they had ever witnessed a hanging. All but three had done so, yet had themselves been undeterred.

Add to this the fact that wherever and whenever capital punishment for murder has been abolished or abandoned, abolition has not been followed by any immediate and perceptible increase in the homicide rate, and the deterrent argument is reduced almost to impotence. Almost; but the deterrent argument is rarely *heard*. Most often the statistics will be listened to with a stubborn incredulity and dismissed as unreliable and irrelevant. "You can prove anything by statistics," the man in the street will mutter to himself. And there's no more to be said. Or rather, there's much more to be said, but there's little point in saying it; for it will be heard with deaf ears.

One of the most moving speeches I ever remember reading was that in 1964 of Henry Brooke, erstwhile Conservative Home Secretary, who in the course of his two years as Home Secretary, changed his mind on this subject, not least because of the statistics.

A rare man indeed to change his mind on this subject; and a rarer to give public utterance to that change.

Nevertheless, it must be said that only thirty years ago, in the House of Lords, Law Lord after Law Lord and Elder Statesman after Elder Statesman, affirmed that capital punishment was an indispensable deterrent to murder. It wasn't only the man in the street who received the statistical argument with incredulity. And to some at least of the distinguished peers who spoke — the then Lord Chief Justice, for instance — it is fair to say that any argument for total abolition was highly unwelcome. The simple fact was, and still is for some, that they would feel deeply unsatisfied and frustrated if certain diabolically wicked murderers were to escape that destruction they seemed so richly to merit. And what is clearly the case is that what often seems like the deterrent argument is barely subconsciously a reliance on the argument from retribution. The death penalty gives the murderer his due. He has deserved to die. It is *Measure for Measure*. He has asked for it, and got it. He has reaped what he has sown. To fare at the hands of others as you have done to others is just and makes sense. It is an eye for an eye. It is justice, even if it is rough justice.

But we do not now maim a man because he has maimed another, or burn a man because he has burnt another. Why, one wonders, should we now kill a man who has killed another? Why should we pay this *particular* type of evil-doer the compliment of imitation?

In fact, the mover of the rejection of Mr. Sydney Silverman's Bill for abolition said literally that "he refused to believe" that for the professional criminal hanging is not a deterrent. And that phrase, "I refuse to believe", was clearly, on that occasion, more than a figure of speech.

But here again the perspective of history is important. To demand an eye for an eye does not exemplify justice; it is primitive justice that does but crudely foreshadow the treatment which enlightened justice requires.

And the perspective of history needs further to be related to retributive capital punishment. It is only for the crime of murder that capital punishment is seriously advocated in Great Britain today. But when Romilly and his friends sought to abolish the death penalty for other crimes, they could appeal to popular sentiment and could demand that penal law should be adapted to the moral and religious sentiments of the nation. It is, of course, easy to be too far ahead of the nation's sentiments. It is as easy to fail to give the moral and religious lead to those sentiments that the times require.

In 1948 Lord Chief Justice Goddard maintained that public opinion is entitled to "the satisfaction of its righteous anger", and that some murders are so shocking, and their perpetrators so bestial, that these must be destroyed.

Public opinion and righteous anger are both notoriously difficult categories to handle. Sir Travers Humphreys used to point out that a man may shoot a mad dog unemotionally, as a work of necessity, because reason tells him it is dangerous. But he grinds the head of a snake with his heel in deep repugnance and antipathy. Mad dogs and snakes may be equally dangerous, but man does not find them equally revolting. The public's righteous anger, which can be vindictiveness and revenge but thinly disguised, is surely not something to which free rein should be given. "We never feel so good as when we are punishing someone," said Bertrand Russell; and there is at least some truth in that statement which dare not be ignored.

And the "bestiality" of the murderer: the word is important. It is easy to use such arguments as though we were discussing a beast and not a man; a thing and not a person; someone no longer an end in himself, who has forfeited the basic right to live, totally, irretrievably and once and for all. He is to be destroyed in the interest of public health, removed as a piece of human carrion or a centre of infection, just as a surgeon cuts out a malignant tumour from a patient's body. But there are few who have been in constant personal touch with prisoners in the condemned cell who find these categories adequate, or, indeed, exalting, to those who use them.

Nevertheless, the argument that subordinates the individual to the needs of society: that is to say, to the needs of the many individuals who make up that society; the argument that it is necessary sometimes for "one man to die for the people", has obvious power: the death that is a warning to others: a symbol to society. "Executions are intended to draw spectators," said Dr. Johnson; "if they do not, they do not answer their purpose". The murderer incurs not simply death, but death in disgrace: death *as* disgrace. "The conscience of the community would be revolted if the criminal were allowed to live," said J.R. Clynes, Home Secretary in 1929.

To none of us is the symbolism of judgment unimportant, yet it's odd how little attention we give today to what I will call the "liturgy" by which society can properly show not only its rejection of the act of murder but also its desire that the murderer shall be reclaimed and retrieved.

In 1786 a man was executed at Bolton for stealing thirty yards of cloth valued at 2/- from Mr. Tweet's bleaching ground. The employers of the neighbourhood had their servants and workpeople assembled to witness the spectacle, and on the following Sunday, the Revd. E. Whitehead, Vicar of Bolton, improved the occasion by preaching a sermon on the recent execution. Nowadays we are so aware of the brutalising effect of public horrors, and of the blood lust which is so easily stirred up in the public when a murderer is on the run, that we give up any imaginative attempt publicly to express the truth of rejection of the murderer, and, equally, any attempt to convey the truth that rejection is not the last word.

Which leads me to *my* last word. Some of you may have thought that my sermon, which has really been about how society maintains its ideals, would really have been more appropriately delivered as a speech in Gray's Inn Debating Society. I would want to insist that to discuss how our society maintains its ideals is a deeply religious occupation. But I would also want to underline that Jesus himself did not die a natural death. He suffered the death penalty for what looks uncommonly like the charge of terrorism. Yet his life, I would claim, did more than any other to provide worthwhile goals not only for the life of the individual but also for society. He of all people taught us the sacredness of human life, and that none of us have the right utterly to eclipse that sacred spark within us; nor should any of us give up trying to fan that spark into a flame, even in the most unpromising person; for there, but for the grace of God, goes each one of us. We dare not admit defeat in the task of reclaiming and restoring this person and that from whatever evil he or she has fallen into, for our religion teaches us that Christ himself lived and died to reclaim not some sorts of sinners but all sorts.

Capital Punishment is an admission of defeat: an admission of irretrievable, irrevocable defeat — of the power of Christ's love in itself, and in us whom he has called to share with him his saving and redeeming work.

It is a profoundly Christian sentiment that Portia expressed, dressed, significantly, like a doctor of laws, when she said that:

> earthly power doth then show
> likest God's
> When mercy seasons justice.

HONOUR EVERYONE

Gray's Inn Chapel: November 18th 1979

"Honour everyone; love the brotherhood; fear God; honour the king."
1 Peter 2 v.17.

You must thank — or blame — Master Gibbens* for my sermon this morning. It was after service last Sunday that he said he found it difficult to "take" the phrase that comes in the blessing I always use at the end of the service: "Go forth into the world in peace; be of good courage; hold fast that which is good; render to no one evil for evil; strengthen the fainthearted; support the weak . . . *Honour everyone*"; and he cited certain of the people he had had up before him of late, and has had to sentence, and asked, understandably, "Do you really expect me to honour such men?" It was a worthwhile question.

To begin to formulate some sort of an answer I would like to indulge in a kind of guessing game. I want to tell you about someone, but leave you to guess whom I'm talking about!

His mother lavished love upon him. His father was a Customs officer, strict, exacting, and unapproachable, who often whipped his son. As a child, the boy particularly loved to play "Cowboys and Indians". He was brought up as a devout Catholic, and delighted in the splendour and solemnity of the church festivals. For a time he wanted to be a priest. He was taken to his first opera when he was a boy of twelve, and it wasn't long before he knew the whole of Wagner's *Ring* almost by heart. He was an above average pianist, and wrote several plays and the libretto of an opera. Bernard Shaw's *St. Joan* was one of his favourite plays. When he left school he often went to concerts with his great friend, whose boys he offered to

* His Honour Judge Brian Gibbens 1912-1985

41

educate when later in life he — my subject — made his name. His father died when he was thirteen. His mother died of cancer when he was eighteen. In the last weeks of her life her son did most of the nursing, and drew a picture of her on her death-bed. He said to the doctor who attended her that he would be grateful to him for the rest of his life, and he kept his word, according him special favours when he was in a position to do so. He wanted to become a student in the great Academy of Art in the main city of his land, but a year's preparatory study on his own ended with the rejection of his application. He often went hungry. For a couple of years he was virtually destitute, living in doss houses, and making what money he could by selling postcard views of city scenes he had sketched and painted. By good fortune, in 1910 an aunt withdrew her savings from the bank, and gave her twenty-one year old nephew a good deal of it. He got good lodgings, and began to work solidly in watercolours and oils, and sold everything he completed to dealers. Poverty and need had turned the young artist into rather a radical in political terms; but with the outbreak of war there wasn't time for art or politics. He joined up, and was soon thrown into the battle of Ypres. His courage knew no bounds, and he won high military decorations for bravery. He was gassed and temporarily blinded. When the war ended, he was thirty.

With the end of the Great War, and unemployed, he took up politics again. A spell in prison was as creative for him as it was for John Bunyan, and he occupied himself with reading and writing. Out of prison, recognition quickly came to him. On his fiftieth birthday the Pope sent him congratulations; and the cardinal ordered a Te Deum to be sung in the local cathedral when he narrowly escaped death at the hands of a would-be assassin. He was able to say to the end: "I am a Catholic, and will always remain so".

Four women attempted suicide for love of him — three successfully; but he didn't in fact marry until shortly before his death. He was always particularly good with the children of his immediate circle of friends; and, just before he died he had some of his friends' children with him.

I expect you've guessed whom I've had in mind: Adolf Hitler.

And I've given you this very selective biography of him, because I have never known anyone myself, no matter how lawless, no matter how sinful, who hasn't had what we call "redeeming features". And PANTAS TIMESATE — "honour everyone" — does not mean ignore what is evil about people; it lays down the obligation of the respect and courtesy due to human personality as such: an obligation which is inconsistent, in the political sphere, with those principles of absolute or totalitarian government, such as National Socialism, which sacrifice the individual wholly to the state; and inconsistent, in the economic sphere, with all systems and methods which regard people simply as "hands", mere cogs in a machine.

Behind those words "honour everyone", lies the belief that, if God is our creator, nothing we can do can entirely deface his image in us. Nothing can entirely remove that in us which is worthy of honour; or, indeed, that which may one day be restored to what it was always intended to be.

When Polonius has said to Hamlet, "I will use them according to their desert", Shakespeare makes Hamlet reply: "God's bodikins, man, much better; use every man after his desert, and who should 'scape whipping? Use them after your own honour and dignity: the less they deserve, the more merit is in your bounty. Take them in."

One of my heroes is John Leonard Wilson, Bishop of Singapore during the Second World War, whom, later, I got to know as a friend. Before he died, he preached in the Sunday Service of the BBC and gave an account of what it meant to him to suffer many weary hours of beatings and torture by the Japanese when he was in prison.

"I did not like to use the words, 'Father, forgive them'", he wrote. "It seemed blasphemous to use Our Lord's words; but I *felt* them . . . When I muttered 'forgive them', I wondered how far I was being dramatic, and if I really meant it; because I looked at their faces as they stood round, taking it in turns to flog me, and their faces were hard and cruel, and some of them were evidently enjoying their cruelty. But, by the grace of God, I saw these men not as they were, but as they had been. Once they were little children, with their brothers and sisters — happy in their parents' love, in those far-off days before they had been conditioned by their false nationalistic ideals. And it is hard to hate little children. So I saw them not as they were, but as they were capable of becoming, redeemed by the power of Christ, and I knew that I should say, 'Forgive'".

When John Leonard Wilson went back to visit Singapore after the war, he told me that one of his greatest joys was to confirm a number of the Japanese who had taken part in flogging him in Changi Gaol.

I have left till last any direct reference to the Gospels and to the life of Christ.

Jesus does not condone the woman taken in adultery; but he is courteous towards her and shows her respect as a human being. He "honours" her, in that sense of the word.

When he tells the story of the Prodigal Son, we are not given many details of the way in which the Prodigal wasted his substance in the far country; but certainly there is no suggestion that there are some states of being, some actions, from which it would have been impossible for the Prodigal to return, or impossible for the father to receive him had he decided to return. But the Prodigal acknowledged his sin, and confessed. Would the Lord have us honour the man or woman who shows no signs of a change of heart?

To me, perhaps the most moving scene in the whole New Testament is when Judas comes with a crowd, with swords and staves, and betrays Jesus to them with a kiss. What does Jesus say to his betrayer? Does he *dis*honour him? Does he refrain from honouring him? He says to him: "Friend, wherefore art thou come?"

The commentary on that verse in the beautiful 14th Century book of German mystical writings *Theologia Germanica*, is: "He said to Judas, when he betrayed him: 'Friend, wherefore art thou come?' Just as if he had said: 'Thou hatest me, and art mine enemy, yet I love thee and am thy friend'. As though God in human nature were saying: 'I am pure, simple Goodness, and therefore I cannot will or desire or rejoice in, or do or give anything but goodness. If I am to reward thee for thy evil and wickedness, I must do it with goodness, for I am and have nothing else."

That is to me the very basis of our honouring not just good people, whoever they may be, but *everyone*.

GOD'S SPIES
Gray's Inn Chapel: November 25th 1979

This evening I have to preach at the University Church at Cambridge, Great St. Mary's. I was asked for my subject many months ago, and said it would be "God's spies"; and that I'd preach on those marvellous lines in *King Lear*:

> To take upon's the mystery of things
> As if we were God's spies.

I'd hoped to preach on that as the task of every one of us. But with the unmasking this week of Anthony Blunt, whom I knew at Trinity College when he was an Honorary Fellow, what I want to say on that subject is now very different.

What is it, I wonder, which makes espionage such a curiously engrossing subject? What is it about it that sends a *frisson* down one's spine: that gives us all, sometimes, even a love-hate relationship with the spy? — even, I suspect, those of you who from time to time are called to sit in judgment upon those who are charged with spying.

Is it too far-fetched, I wonder, to suggest that it's in part because the spy is a man of two worlds? And as the man who pre-eminently has to be dealt with by "Security", he becomes the living symbol — maybe more than the symbol — of that struggle with insecurity which is our human condition? The spy story becomes *par excellence* the extended image, the myth, of mystery at the heart of things.

Put it this way: you never know with the spy which country he's really working for: to which country he really belongs. You can say where he began; but you're never entirely certain where he'll end up. Part of him belongs beyond the horizon, and underlines any uncertainty we might have about where we belong; and, thus threatened, we become of a sudden Jingoistic in defence of the land of our birth. We become this worldly, so to speak, just because the spy reminds us of Another Country: and of its principalities and powers.

I've suddenly found myself in these last weeks wanting to write my own spy story — "Tinker, tailor, soldier, priest" — about a Christ-figure of a spy, so evidently a man of two worlds that he reminds every other human being that they are — we are — men of two worlds: the Christ-figure who comes from Another Country, but while he's amongst us could never have looked more human, with a face like all men's faces; could never have been more human, yet his loyalty transcends this world. Jesus, the double agent, undergoing the "double agony" — "in man, for man". Jesus, the Man who comes in — not from the Cold (God help us!) — but from, certainly, the Beyond: from, as I say, Another Country; from, if you like, the Warm. Not, of course, the Mole; but maybe, the Lamb — or even the Lion.

And His Crucifixion? I'd want to explore that from the angle of what people want to do, and, in the end, succeed in doing, to the Man Who Knew Too Much. Which is probably a good point to say something about motivation.

Anthony Blunt has said, not entirely convincingly, that his motivation was his conscience. I don't want to comment on that statement in itself. (It will be no surprise to you that I am not in possession of any special facts that could confirm or refute that statement.) But whatever else is *not* clear, it *is* clear, surely, that a spy has to be strongly motivated, be it a political motive, or cash, or revenge, or whatever: it has to be something which from within is compelling, and eminently worthwhile. Whatever motive could make a man risk the possibility of remaining amongst his friends; risk the whole of his future career; even life itself? A spy, without doubt, has to be exceedingly strongly motivated, even if that strong motivation may seem from one angle primarily negative, like the overthrow of one's own country.

So let me, in passing, ask a question about motivation today. Am I right to be worried that those at our universities, many say, can be divided into those who are strongly motivated and those who "don't give a damn"? And that those who "don't give a damn" — about the future of society, for instance: whether it's communist or fascist, or whether that two-thirds of the world which is hungry continues to be hungry or is fed — form quite a large proportion of undergraduates and graduates. I find myself asking isn't no motivation almost as worrying as wrong motivation?

Yesterday I was visiting someone with leukaemia in a London hospital. Several of the beds in the ward were unoccupied, as they are in several wards. Why? Because, I was told, of "cuts". I am myself very worried that so few people seem to be concerned about the cuts in the Health Service. It's certainly not just the motivation of *students* which concerns me.

Anthony Blunt claimed that conscience was his motive. And one daily paper, quoting Trevor-Roper, responded with the headline: "Damn your conscience!". I want to say: "Let that paper, let that person, whoever says 'Damn your conscience', itself — himself — be damned — if the conscience of the one he's addressing is a sincere conscience which that person has taken care to inform to the very best of his ability."

If at the moment there was someone in Russia who as a matter of conscience could not support the Soviet way of life; and if that man had the possibility of overthrowing or assisting the overthrow of Soviet Russia, would we not say: "What courage, what bravery, that risked life and limb to secure that downfall"? It's either right to follow an informed conscience or not right. It cannot be right to follow it in Russia and wrong to follow it in Great Britain.

But surely it's the nature of the motivation that counts. Any old motivation will not do.

One of my heroes is Dietrich Bonhoeffer. His involvement in the conspiracy against Hitler involved first a weight of dangerous and detailed secret knowledge which fomented searching questions in his conscience. And as he became more and more enmeshed in the evil necessities of his time, he was driven quietly to accept the loss of that particular personal treasure which he had many times struggled to abandon, but which had clung to him, wrapping its powerful tentacles round his inmost being: the sense of his own righteousness. That maggot at the heart of the rose was eventually removed — but that was the *outcome*, not the motivation, of his involvement. Yet at least Bonhoeffer wasn't a self-righteous traitor.

In ten days time I go to Calcutta. I have been invited to a conference that will look at its "bustees", and look at its facts of life, and will have to recommend the kind of Aid which Calcutta needs, must have, in the 80's; and the way it should be given; and comment upon the kind of socio-political and economic set-up which is to be desired for that to happen. You will remember: a General Election in India will take place in January.

I wonder what kind of political and economic set-up you would be willing to work for, give your life for, that people in Calcutta might have a life worth living? And I wonder what kind of political and economic set-up over here in Great Britain and Europe you think that implies? And I wonder what kind of action you are willing to take to see that we in Britain give the kind of help you judge we should give? Would you ever see yourself in conscience bound to work for the overthrow of a government that fills the rich with good things and sends the poor empty away?

Do you, I wonder, think that Capitalism can solve India's problems? Or Communism? Or what alternative have you in mind?

And would you offer your answer as an opinion, or would you be willing to back that opinion, to commit yourself to an answer — and what would you mean by commitment? It was, after all, commitment to a particular answer to the problem of society in the Thirties which was the motivation which Blunt *said* lay behind his actions.

To go back to my Christ-figure. If he really were to be a Christ-figure-sort-of-spy, his motivation would have to be compassion, love, service, and the desire to see each human being reach his full potential; and the measure of his commitment would have to have something about it that echoed that so well-known verse:

> And in the garden secretly
> And on the Cross on high
> Should teach his brethren and inspire
> To suffer and to die.

But there is, of course, no spy story worthy of the name without the possibility of betrayal. There must always be a Judas figure — or two — or four . . .

But before we isolate Judas, I think we need to look at the mob: those who encourage the headline writers: the witch-hunters: those who have more interest in the circulation than in the truth. The crowd that cries "Damn your conscience" is itself guilty of high treason: of betraying the very royalty of human nature itself. In my Christ-figure story there'd have to be people who, when asked would they stay by him as his friends, would say: "I know not the man"; and there'd be Hosannas that change all too quickly into "Crucify!".

My spy story would probably be a failure, because in a spy story you have to keep the tension going right till the end; and I don't think I'd be able to conceal for long the soft spot I've always had for Judas.

I cannot forget that remarkable essay of Graham Greene called "The Lost Childhood", and the lines he quotes at its end from "Germinal", a poem of the Irish poet, "A.E.":

> In ancient shadows and twilights
> Where childhood had strayed
> The world's great sorrows were born
> And its heroes were made.
> In the lost childhood of Judas
> Christ was betrayed.

Many people have mentioned Anthony Blunt's days as an undergraduate in Cambridge. Very few have mentioned his boyhood, except to say his father was a parson, in London, behind the Edgware Road.

But why should we except the spy from other delinquents: from other Judases? Hardly a tear was shed for George Blake, the spy. He was a spy — but he was half a foreigner and half a Jew. No need, people said, to waste any tears on *him*. And Vassall? — another parson's son: he was written off as a social upstart and "gay". And Burgess and Maclean? Le Carré calls them "psychiatric misfits" and thinks no more need therefore be said. And Philby? Le Carre calls him "An aggressive upper class enemy. He was of our blood and hunted with our pack; to the very end, he expected and received the indulgence owing to his moderation, good breeding and boyish flirtatious charm." Yes; but why do we except him and the other spies from other delinquents?

I can never forget that when I was Chaplain of Trinity, one of my best undergraduate friends, who came up with a scholarship; whose mother, to whom he was greatly attached, died in his first week in Cambridge; who went out to Hungary when the rising there took place; who came back and preached in Great St. Mary's, to a church crowded to the galleries, when he went down from Cambridge — without a degree — got through a small fortune in his first year and was imprisoned for hiring cars in one country and selling them in others. (He was a very skilled lad!) When I met him when he came out of prison I asked him what he had most hated about it. He said immediately. "The way one kind of prisoner would be cruel to another — the bank robbers to the sex criminals, for instance . . . You would have thought that by then we would have learnt to have pity on one another." That young man helped to teach me that there's usually a hidden reason behind the deeds of those we conveniently label "Judas".

When I went from being Chaplain of Trinity to be Vicar of the Trinity College Mission in South London we were proud to have based within the parish a major pioneer research project into delinquency, under the auspices of the Cambridge Institute of Criminology. Four hundred local boys were studied for eight years, from the age of eight to sixteen, to observe the onset of delinquent behaviour and explore the factors which distinguished the delinquent minority from their fellows. The research was able to identify fairly accurately a vulnerable minority, characterised in the main by poor academic achievement and adverse family influences. That research is now published in three volumes, *Present Conduct and Future Delinquency*. But society does not take much notice of such research. We pay for it; we pay verbal tribute to it; but it is as though the judge, the magistracy and the police, simply dare not face what living alongside and carefully studying the delinquent reveals. And I see no reason why spies — whether they come from a public school and upper class background, like Blunt and Philby — or from a working class background — should be excepted from what we have to say about delinquency in general.

Yet when a boy of twenty — like, for instance, Kim Philby — gives himself body and mind to a country he has never visited, to an ideology he could not have understood from within, to a régime which even abroad, during those long and awful purges, was a peril to serve; when he remains actively faithful to that decision for over thirty years, cheating, betraying and occasionally killing; we dare not underestimate the nature and depth of that delinquency. Nothing I have said, therefore, will, I hope, be taken to diminish what I believe to be the seriousness of what is done by the traitor.

It is, in fact, the evil of what is done which would provide the challenge to any man writing a Christ-figure spy story. It would have to have some hint in it of the profundity of Christ's redemption. You may know those lines of Edwin Muir's poem, "The Transfiguration":

> Then he will come, Christ the uncrucified,
> Christ the discrucified, his death undone,
> His agony unmade, his cross dismantled —
> Glad to be so — and the tormented wood
> Will cure its hurt and grow into a tree
> In a green springing corner of young Eden,
> And Judas damned take his long journey backward
> From darkness into light and be a child
> Beside his mother's knee, and the betrayal
> Be quite undone and never more be done.

In my story, the Christ-figure double-agent would need somehow to undo and redeem what has been done; it can't be sufficient just to leave the mess as it is.

The Mess. I suppose one of the most distressing features of the Anthony Blunt case has been the attempt to say, "Well, it's all a long while ago; so why not just forget it? Does it really matter all that much? He was very good on Poussin!" I find that distressing; because if you take away the significance of good and evil you take away much of the significance of life itself — and, indeed, of much of the greatest art. If you pretend that suffering caused to others is not important, it's not long before nothing matters.

It's important, therefore, to see the Anthony Blunt affair against the backcloth of good and evil. Tear down that backcloth and you destroy the fabric of the world. With that backcloth, which takes seriously good and evil, we shall not be tempted to forget and pass over the past, and we shall be led to explore how to purge it. Not to forget, but to forgive: a far more profound undertaking.

And yet that's not where I want to leave things.

It is clear that it's necessary in England now to see at least some of the recent rash of spies against the political background of the 30's — Burgess, Maclean, Philby, Blunt. Not many people are convinced that that will explain all: to see Philby, for instance, simply as a ruthless and determined Communist. But in England now it is for us to come out of the story of espionage in the past and say what we will do with the present. If Philby, Blunt and Burgess and Maclean decided to be Communists — for whatever reason — that is one thing. But it still leaves us with our decisions.

Shortly after Christmas I shall be in Sri Lanka, staying for part of the time with a good Sri Lankan friend of mine, a priest and graduate of Cambridge University, on a collective farm that has become a centre for Buddhist-Christian-Marxist dialogue. The Christ-figure I shall take with me there, in my heart and mind, isn't only a Saviour figure. He's not only a person concerned with individuals. He's concerned with the structures of society. He's concerned with standing alongside the poor in their struggle for justice.

There are not all that many people who would see now in Russian Communism hope for Sri Lanka and India. Not many of us would now be tempted to defect with Blunt. Yet I want to say that "God's spies" are always on the look-out for how and where His kingdom may come: always aware that their loyalty to Christ has to be put above loyalty to family, to friends, to country.

Yes: I think those of us who confess and call ourselves Christians have to "take upon's the mystery of things as if we were God's spies." But that will mean taking upon us the Mystery of Good and Evil, and of how Evil can be redeemed: how Good can be brought out of Evil:

in this person and that:
in this society and that;
by this means and that.

And, in the end, *our* loyalty is with Another Country.

LADY ISOBEL BARNETT

Gray's Inn Chapel: November 16th 1980

Many of us are unlikely to forget the name of Isobel Barnett as long as we live. Her suicide has touched us all.

Yet now the inquest is over and the cause of her death established, I think it may be fruitful — that is: some good may even be brought out of evil — if we reflect awhile on some aspects of that sad story.

In the British Medical Journal for the 11th September 1971 there is the summary of a ten-year follow-up of 886 shoplifters: the results of a study by the then Professor of Forensic Psychiatry at the Institute of Psychiatry, Professor Gibbens, and his two research assistants; a study supported by the Nuffield Foundation.

That study underlined the extreme differences between men and women shoplifters: the men tended to have previous convictions, and to steal books; 80% of the women were first offenders and none of them stole books. A third of the women were foreign born, and mostly aged between 17 and 30. The peak age among British women was 51 to 60. The rate of admission to hospital for the women shoplifters was three times higher than average.

What the study also underlined is the stereotyped attitudes to shoplifting. Psychiatrists, for instance, will stress that some respectable and usually late middle-aged women shoplift for neurotic reasons and with minimal motive of gain. And that attitude is well accepted by *women* magistrates, who can obviously more easily identify with such unfortunate women: but it is not so easily accepted by *men* magistrates. And shop managers and detectives are more likely to draw attention to the large amount of casual shoplifting for simple gain.

The problem, you will know well enough, is to place offenders justly along "the continuum, from the casually dishonest to the pathological."

52

I have also been studying the Hertfordshire Shoplifting Survey. In one year, all the women probation officers in the county worked together on a group study of shoplifting. 130 cases were studied, which represents probably only a very small proportion of the total number of women who shoplifted from Hertfordshire stores that year. And probably a considerable number of those who were caught were those with over-riding problems and anxieties: others would have been better able to make their get-away.

But why do I think this subject is appropriate for a sermon in this chapel?

I suppose, first of all, because all of us here, in one way and another, as part of our Christian vocation, are concerned with and for justice. It is worrying, for instance, if the justice meted out by a male magistrate is different because of his maleness from that which would be meted out by a female magistrate.

Secondly, what Professor Gibbens' survey called "the continuum from the casually dishonest to the pathological" indicates an intractable problem which, surely, we have to go on working at. If women are ever *in custody* for acts that are *pathological* in origin, that is very worrying; or if anyone is convicted for an act that is primarily pathological and is a potential suicide, that, too, is very worrying indeed.

Lady Isobel Barnett said, after she had been convicted, "I can't stop stealing things. I know I have a serious problem." She spoke of the "private hell" she had been living in for years. But in court, as you know, she maintained her innocence to the last.

There is something there, too, which is an appropriate subject for a sermon in our Chapel. It was tragic that no one seemed able to win Isobel Barnett's confidence sufficiently for her to unburden herself and tell them the whole story. That surely says something to us all, and is perhaps a warning to us all: it speaks of the mask that is the blessing to so many of us who have to perform in public — which is, at times, at crucial times, curse as well. There can be few more tragic stories than this story of someone who did such a lot to make so many of us so happy; who was a practising doctor for seven years — and a magistrate. She saved others: herself she could not save.

One of the privileges of a priest's life is that he's often called upon to minister to those who have been able to pluck up their courage to ask for help. I don't think now I'd be surprised at anything anyone told me about themselves. I've been told too often by someone of the double life they've been helplessly living. And the more public responsibility they've had, the more the mask has often become part of them. In fact I'd go so far as to say that this Jekyll and Hyde existence — of, for instance, Lady Isobel — is only a matter of degree. That doesn't mean I underrate the "private hell" that some people live in, maybe because of some compulsive acts they're repeatedly driven to: some sexual act, or drinking habit, or some petty smash and grab raid, like shoplifting. Many such actions, I'm convinced, are grabbing at the symbol of something else. They're the actions of people desperately hungry for love and valuation, with the accent on the word "desperate"; and such actions are almost always much more akin to sickness than to sin, though they cause mountains of self-rejection and guilt.

I can't forget one of my fellow clergy who was had up for shoplifting in Oxford Street. He didn't need what he stole and had a full wallet on him. Clearly he was a sick man. He was convicted. He went to the court on the first day of the Diocese's clergy conference. The Bishop of the Diocese made a point of sitting next to him at table that first evening of the Conference and made immediate arrangements for him to see a psychiatrist. After three years' treatment the priest decided he himself wanted to be a priest-psychotherapist — which he is now — and an enormous help to many. Good has been brought out of evil.

So often one side of ourselves — the priestly side, the good side — needs by the grace of God to say to the other side of ourselves, to the dark side within us, the bit of ourselves we cannot accept, what the priestly Prospero says to the savage, deformed Caliban: "This thing of darkness I acknowledge mine". The tragedy of Isobel Barnett is that this side of the grave, it seems, she was unable to say that; and, it seems, no one was found to help her say it. But the end of our life in this world is not the end of the world of God's love. For myself, I believe Isobel Barnett will have found now the love, the mercy and the justice she was seeking: at which she was grabbing. Indeed, the merciful, loving and just Lord, I believe, will credit her with desire for the Love that he is, even in what, this side of the grave, looked to us simply like a hand outstretched for a tin of tuna fish and a pot of cream, value 87p. And may that love, mercy and justice, which is known beyond the grave to Isobel Barnett, be made known in the here and now to us, in our need, whatever that may be, now, and always.

A SUPREME EXAMPLE OF JUDGMENT

Gray's Inn Chapel: November 23rd 1980

The fact that every man's a judge in no way denies society's need of particular people to be judges. And the particular people who are called to be judges in society, focus and clarify the gift and responsibility that is given to every human being to judge. Similarly, there are certain judgments that need to be made by the generality of men and women which highlight the particular gift of judgment that is given to us all.

A supreme example of such a judgment is surely what we human beings do with and about what we now call "the Bomb". We can all agree that this judgment highlights the amazing gift and responsibility that has been given humanity for good and ill.

I want to preach to you about this particular example of judgment, which belongs to us all, in a way which avoids unnecessary and unprofitable controversy; so I shall simply tell you something about the man from whom I personally have learnt most about "the Bomb": a man in whom this gift and responsibility of judgment on behalf of all humanity was focused at a particular time in particular decisions.

Otto Frisch was a refugee in this country from Nazi Germany. I used often to sit next to him at meals at Trinity College, Cambridge. He seemed to relish invitations to meet undergraduates and talk with them. He would gladly let the Chaplains interview him to draw him out. He was extremely entertaining company: brilliant on the piano, but as brilliant at drawing sketches of his friends in a few seconds — but not only his friends!

Frisch was born in Vienna; his grandfather was a Polish Jew. His mother was a pianist and composer. His father was a printer and publisher.

Otto, as a child, was a bit of a mathematical prodigy, though the piano and music were almost as important to him. At the University of Vienna he turned to Physics first and Mathematics second, and gained his doctorate at twenty-two. Out of University, he was soon given a job in Berlin, with people like the Nobel Prize winner Max Planck, and, occasionally, Einstein.

It was when Frisch was in Hamburg, at the Department of Physical Chemistry, that Hitler came to power, in the early Thirties. Otto would admit that when Hitler was making speeches and starting a party he paid no attention. He said to himself, "I'm a physicist. I'll get on with my science", though he began to pay a bit more attention when Hitler's opposition to the Jews turned out to be more than talk. He said that when some of his friends told him about concentration camps, and synagogues burnt, and beatings, and torture, he just couldn't believe that Germans could do that kind of thing.

In the summer of 1933, Niels Bohr, the Danish genius and Director of the Institute for Theoretical Physics there, invited Frisch to Copenhagen, to help him to escape from Nazi Germany and find a job abroad. So that year Frisch came to London. He said that one thing surprised him in England: his English colleagues knew a lot more about politics, literature and sport, than their German counterparts. He said that what he had learnt was that the knowledge of a speciality like physics, or any other, without some understanding of politics and human behaviour, did little to protect the average German from a vicious ideology like Nazism.

At that time, Frisch was only over here for a year. He went back to Niels Bohr and the Institute in Copenhagen for another five years, until the outbreak of the Second World War, when he had to get back smartly to England. In those five years he did important work on the splitting of the uranium nucleus and on neutrons.

If you asked Frisch what he had learnt from Bohr, he would often say that Bohr never trusted a purely formal or mathematical argument. "No, no!" Bohr would say. "You are not *thinking*; you are just being logical. You must *think*! You must *think*! You must *think*!"

Frisch would say that in physics we often speak of "complementarity": of "pairs" which you can accurately observe, but never both at once — like "position" and "speed"; and that he had come to believe there are many "pairs" which are basic to life, which we have to observe separately but keep together — like "body and mind", "matter and life", "justice and mercy". "Reality," he would say, "is painted on both sides of a canvas, so that you can only see one aspect of it clearly at any time; but both aspects of it are important."

Frisch worked in Birmingham for a couple of years, with another German-born mathematical physicist, Rudolf Peierls, later Wykeham Professor of Physics at Oxford. And it was while working there that he did the work which proved that an atomic bomb was possible.

People often asked Frisch: "When you came to that realisation, did you think that it might possibly be right to say nothing to anybody and abandon the project then and there? That it might be hideously wrong to start on a project which, if successful, would end with the production of a weapon of unparalleled violence: a weapon of mass destruction such as the world has never seen?" Frisch would answer, "Really it was simple. We were at war. And if I had come up with the idea, very probably some of my German colleagues still in Germany were working on the same idea, maybe had had it already".

Frisch and Peierls went to one of the pupils of Rutherford, Mark Oliphant, in charge of the laboratory at Birmingham, to tell him why they now believed it was possible to make an atomic bomb. He went to Sir Henry Tizard, the then Scientific Adviser to the Government, and soon Frisch was transferred to Liverpool to get on with his work.

So it happened that in 1943 he was one of a few dozen scientists who were the only passengers on the luxury liner *Andes*, which made a dash across the Atlantic, without convoy, in order to set up a team with American scientists, like Robert Oppenheimer, at Los Alamos, and refugee scientists from many nations, to build the atomic bomb.

I shall never forget Otto Frisch's description of the explosion of the first bomb, at a site code-named "Trinity". He said that before the mushroom cloud, it looked like a "red-hot elephant standing balanced on its trunk".

He said that after the explosion there was a lot of discussion about how to use the weapon. Should it be used at all? Should a demonstration be staged on an uninhabited island with the enemy invited to watch it? He said repeatedly that he was never a natural politician. But he felt he had to argue that to do the right thing with the bomb was of the utmost importance. Quite a lot of people said simply: "Scientists should stick to matters of their own competence." But Frisch was convinced that was an ostrich-like attitude. "Besides," he said, "scientists are trained to think dispassionately and objectively, and the people who can do that are in very short supply in the world today."

Then one day, three weeks after the bomb had been exploded, there was a sudden noise outside Frisch's laboratory, and running footsteps. Someone burst in through his door and said, "Hiroshima has been destroyed: about a hundred thousand people have been killed!"

Frisch said he felt very uneasy — and then he felt sick — when he saw how many of his friends were rushing to the telephone to book tables at the "La Fonda" hotel in Santa Fe in order to celebrate.

"Of course," he said, "it was the climax of their work — and mine — and its success." And perhaps this slaughter had saved the lives of many more Americans and Japanese who would have died in the slow process of conquest by which the war might have had to be ended had there been *no* atomic bomb.

But when a second bomb was dropped on Nagasaki only a few days later, Frisch could see no moral reason for it. This new and terrifying and godlike power seemed to have gone to the heads of those with the power of decision.

Frisch went back to his work, and returned to England, to be head of the nuclear physics division at the Harwell establishment of the Atomic Energy Authority, and then to be Jacksonian Professor of Natural Philosophy and Fellow of Trinity College, Cambridge. He died, at seventy-four, in September this year.

I hope you understand now why I have chosen to preach — or, more accurately, to talk about Otto Frisch.

Whatever we mean by "God", surely he must be behind the gifts of someone like Frisch, which enabled him to identify the nuclear fission of uranium and to realise its explosive possibilities — for good and evil — and to apprehend the question of "not simply being an ostrich-like scientist", but seeing that those gifts must go with the gift of political knowledge and responsibility — and justice and mercy.

I see Otto Frisch's gifts and responsibility of judgment as highlighting and underlining the gifts that are given to all of us. We all have those gifts, and the responsibility of judgment, to some degree.

Such gifts require, surely, conscious co-operation with him who gave them. Or did those gifts simply come out of nowhere and nothing?

We gather here, I hope, and suggest, and believe, because we believe it right to hand back and consecrate our gift of judgment to him, who has given such great gifts to us all.

THE PRODIGAL SON

Gray's Inn Chapel: July 5th 1981

At the Aldeburgh Festival there was recently a revival of Britten's third "church parable' *The Prodigal Son*. He wrote it in 1968, inspired by Rembrandt's painting *The Return of the Prodigal*, which he'd seen in the Hermitage, when he was on a concert tour in Leningrad, earlier in the 60's. Some of you may have seen the *Prodigal Son* panel in the Britten Memorial Window in Aldeburgh Parish Church. John Piper acknowledges that it was the Rembrandt in the Hermitage which was his inspiration.

The test of a really great story is often what it provokes in art, literature and music; and by that test alone the Prodigal Son is certainly great.

It doesn't at all surprise me that André Gide has a story inspired by the Prodigal; that it provoked a Cantata from Debussy and a powerful piece of sculpture from Rodin. And I'd love to have been present when the ballet of the Prodigal opened in Paris in 1929 at the Sarah Bernhardt Theatre, with the music by Prokofiev, the choreography by Balanchine, the sets and the costumes by Rouault, and Diaghilev's Ballets Russes. What an "Evening for Prodigals" it must have been!

I know of no story that is more on the human nerve. We readily perceive it's not simply about someone else, the Prodigal Son, but about Everyman, about ourselves. It's not only a great Bible story; it's one of the great human myths about Man, the Eternal Prodigal. There's no explicit doctrine in it; no mention of God; no sermon. But it's unmistakably about Adam: Man.

The very first phrase establishes an air of anonymity which can include us all. "A certain man had two sons." No name to the father; no name to the sons. It's everyone, everywhere.

And then, in a few phrases, there is unfolded what is familiar to us all in the "growing up process" of ourselves and our children, and of, no doubt, the students here, for whom we have some responsibility and care.

The "process of growing up" always means taking the share of our inheritance: the gifts we're given by our parents and life itself, and at some stage leaving the nest, spreading our wings, and taking off. Often, at that stage, for one reason and another, we grab what we can get, violently, and maybe get cut off from home. It's sad when that time of setting out is a time of pain and strife between parent and child, child and parent; but, as an erstwhile university chaplain, I have come to recognise that that time of strife is almost as natural as its absence.

Some sons, it's true, would like to grab what they can and make off, but haven't the courage, and remain behind, virtue seemingly intact. There used to be an advertisement which had a monk, avidly drinking his pint, and saying "Courage got me into the habit", which always tempted me to write, while no one was looking: "More courage might have got you out of it"! Could it be that the Elder Brother was held back by fear, ensnared by convention and lack of courage? That would acount for some of his anger, jealous anger.

Do you know, I wonder, C. Day Lewis's poem, 'Walking away'?

It is eighteen years ago, almost to the day —
A sunny day with the leaves just turning,
The touch-lines new-ruled — since I watched you play
Your first game of football, then, like a satellite
Wrenched from its orbit, go drifting away

Behind a scatter of boys. I can see
You walking away from me towards the school
With the pathos of a half-fledged thing set free
Into a wilderness, the guilt of one
Who finds no path where the path should be.

That hesitant figure, eddying away
Like a winged seed loosened from its parent stem,
Has something I never quite grasp to convey
About nature's give-and-take — the small, the scorching
Ordeals which fire one's irresolute clay.

I have had worse partings, but none that so
Gnaws at my mind still. Perhaps it is roughly
Saying what God alone could perfectly show —
How selfhood begins with a walking away,
And love is proved in the letting go.

All of us have some sympathy for the Prodigal as he sets out. You can almost hear him whistling and see him swagger. Again; it's Man who's journeying. It's *Homo Viator*, as Gabriel Marcel, the existentialist philosopher, calls him: "Man the Traveller", who's always on a Journey.

Then come those resonant phrases which sound like a bell in fog at sea:

A far country . . . wasted his substance . . . there arose a famine . . . he began to be in want,

and a phrase of incredible pathos: "No man gave unto him".

Adam is now an alien: a stranger in a strange land. He has left the Garden. His vaunted independence begins to look a bit of a sham. His anonymity means that nobody knows and nobody cares. But he has at least home-sickness, longing, nostalgia: *A la Recherche du Temps Perdu*.

But he has no overt religious problem, as far as he knows. He's just fed up, despairing, and hungry. The desire to return has no very high motivation. Yet despair, frustration and guilt bring the Prodigal to himself. "He came to himself" is another wonderfully resonant phrase.

The trivial relationships of the far country awake in him the memory of the constant and profound relationship he had experienced "once upon a time". How lucky — how blessed — the Prodigal was to have had such a relationship, such a memory to recall.

The outward journey involved the longing to be free. The homeward journey involved that longing no less, and probably more: but, once more, it involved an inescapable decision.

Now it's the longing of the Father that adds a new dimension to the picture: it's the constant relationship of the Father, his prodigal love, that lights up Rembrandt's great work.

The Father re-clothes the lost boy. And it's to the Elder Brother that there is the finest articulation of that enduring relationship:

Son, thou art ever with me;
    and all that I have is thine.

What more shall we say of that Elder Brother, who, when everyone was piping, would not dance?

Do you know Kipling's poem of the Prodigal, in *Kim*, which tells us quite a bit about Kipling, and maybe also about his love for India, his "Far Country":

Here come I to my own again,
Fed, forgiven and known again,
Claimed by bone of my bone again
And cheered by flesh of my flesh.

The fatted calf is dressed for me,
But the husks have greater zest for me.
I think my pigs will be best for me,
So I'm off to the Yards afresh.

I never was very "refined" you see,
(And it weighs on my brother's mind, you see)
But there's no reproach among swine, d'you see,
For being "a bit of a swine".
So I'm off — with wallet and staff — to eat
The bread that is three parts chaff to wheat,
But glory be! — there's a laugh to it,
Which isn't the case when we dine.

My father glooms and advises me,
My brother sulks and despises me
And Mother catechises me
Till I want to go out and swear.
And, in spite of the butler's gravity,
I know that the servants have it I
Am a "monster of moral depravity",
And I'm damned if I think it's fair!
I wasted my substance, I know I did,
On riotous living, so I did,
But there's nothing on record to show I did
More than my better's have done.
They talk of the money I spent out there —
They hint at the pace I went out there —
But they all forget I was sent out there
Alone, as a rich man's son.

So I was a mark for plunder at once,
And lost my cash (can you wonder?) at once,
But I didn't give up and knock under at once.
I worked in the Yards, for a spell,
Where I spent my nights and my days with hogs,
And shared their milk and maize — with hogs!!
Till I guess I have learned what pays with hogs
And I have that knowledge to sell!!

So back I go to my job again,
Not so easy to rob again,
Or quite so ready to sob again
On any neck that's around.
I'm leaving! Pater. Good-bye to you!
God bless you, Mater! I'll write to you . . .
I wouldn't be impolite to you . . .
But, Brother, you are a Hound!

What a story! — that's 2,000 years old, and yet can go on provoking artist after artist, including Kipling at the turn of the century. I hear there's a Scott Joplin Ballet of the Prodigal now. What a story! — that, after 2,000 years, can go on speaking to you and me.

What a story about the Human Condition — and what a Story Teller to have told such a tale!

I doubt whether any judge or magistrate — or any parent, for that matter — can afford not to refresh their mind and memory from time to time by reading again and reflecting upon that story of the Prodigal. But let me remind you what I said at the beginning: The Prodigal is not about *other* people — ne'er-do-wells; It's about you and me.

BEFORE A ROYAL WEDDING

Gray's Inn Chapel: July 26th 1981

You probably now know that there's going to be a royal wedding next Wednesday!

To my mind, it's a cause for thankfulness that the bride and bridegroom have chosen as one of the hymns, when they might have been expected to be totally absorbed in their vows to one another: "I vow to thee, my country".

There's quite a story attached to both the words and the music of that hymn.

Sir Cecil Spring-Rice, who wrote the words, was Ambassador to Washington from 1914 until the United States came into the First World War; then, at the end of 1917, he was suddenly relieved of his post, by telegram. Cecil Spring-Rice had realised from the beginning of the War that its issue might well depend in the last resort on the attitude of America, and how much therefore depended on him as Ambassador during the prolonged period of American hesitation and neutrality; but he had not anticipated that when he had "done his bit" he would be so suddenly, and, as he felt, so discourteously, replaced by a direct representative of the War Cabinet, Lord Reading; though he recognised the advisability of a change.

On January 3rd, 1918, Cecil Spring-Rice had his final interview with President Woodrow Wilson, and on January 12th, the eve of his departure from Washington, still in some bitterness of soul, he penned the two verses of the hymn; though there is evidence he had been thinking along the lines of the verses for some time.

He left Washington to stay for a while in Ottawa with the Governor-General, the Duke of Devonshire, who was a kinsman of his wife, and then to catch the boat home to England.

On January 19th, in Ottawa, he made a speech to the Canadian Club, in the course of which he said: "The world has had many ideals. Two of the most prominent are present in the minds of us all. We have seen the relics of Egypt or Assyria. We have seen the emblem of the ancient religions, the ancient monarchies — the king on his throne, the badge of sovereignty in his hand, the scourge. We have read of the ruins of a palace once decorated with pictures of burning cities, troops of captives being tortured to death. That was the banquet hall of the King of Assyria. That is one type of civilisation."

"There is another", he went on, "the sign of which is the Cross. I need not tell you what that means, but I must say this: the Cross is a sign of patience under suffering, but not patience under wrong. The Cross is on the banner under which we fight — the Cross of St. George, the Cross of St. Andrew, the Cross of St. Patrick; different in form, in colour, in history, yes, but the same in spirit, the spirit of sacrifice.

We are all subjects of the Prince of Peace, the Prince of Peace who fought the greatest fight ever fought upon this earth, Who won the greatest victory, and won it by His blood . . . That is the Cross . . ."

Only a fortnight after that speech, whilst still in Ottawa, Cecil Spring-Rice suddenly died.

His pension ceased with his death, and his widow was left with little money and two young children to bring up. Mercifully, there was a "Cecil Spring-Rice Memorial Fund" which raised £15,000.

His daughter was sent to St. Paul's School, where the music master was one Gustavus von Holst, born in Gloucestershire, but of Scandinavian, German and Russian forbears. He had recently changed his name to Gustav Holst, much as Prince Charles' forbears, the Battenbergs, changed their name, at the same time, to Mountbatten.

Gustav Holst, who was, of course, becoming a British composer of the first rank, had completed his suite *The Planets* by May 1917, and it was an astonishing coincidence that the melody he had set at the heart of "Jupiter" in *The Planets* fitted, almost without alteration, Spring-Rice's words, which were written many months later, and which were found on his desk in Washington by the Duchess of Devonshire after his death.

There was another not unremarkable coincidence.

Holst had written part of *The Planets* in his 300 year old cottage at Thaxted, in Essex; and he therefore, not surprisingly, called his tune to Spring-Rice's words: "Thaxted".

The Vicar of Thaxted, Conrad Noel, became a great friend of Holst, and Holst was responsible for much of the music-making there. Conrad Noel was a challenging, controversial figure in the Church of England at the time: the life and soul of the Christian Socialists; a vigorous sort of man, with a considerable sense of humour — and drama. It was Gustav Holst's Christian Socialism which had in part drawn him to Thaxted and to Conrad Noel.

Conrad Noel, like Spring-Rice, had strong views on the Union Jack — but rather different ones. Noel feared the Union Jack was too imperialist, and stood most, (I quote), for "financiers, politicians, and newspaper proprietors grown fat upon Empire, and for an Empire which had enlarged its borders by force." It was, of course, one thing to believe that kind of thing, even to say it; but when, after the Easter Rising in Ireland in 1916, Noel added the old flag of Ireland, the Sinn Fein flag, with its golden harp on a deep blue background, to the flags in the chancel at Thaxted, and, later that year, added the Red Flag, to represent, he said "the aspiration of labour for equality of men within the nation, and for a federation of nations within a world commonwealth", it was not only the peacefulness of the village of Thaxted which was shattered.

That was all sixty years ago, and more; and we live now in a rather different world. The Washington in which Spring-Rice wrote his last words is certainly a very different city now. One wonders whether Cecil Spring-Rice could ever have conceived that riots would hit Washington in the 60's, and, indeed, disturbances in 150 cities of the United States, which made President Johnson speak of "a week such as no nation should live through: a time of violence and tragedy"? And could Gustav Holst ever have imagined that his melody from *The Planets* would be used at the wedding of the heir to the throne in the Year of Our Lord 1981, and that there would be riots in a number of English cities in the preceding weeks?

Holst and Spring-Rice certainly lived in a very different world from ours. Yet I myself believe those words of Spring-Rice which Holst set to music may still have within them something of the answer to our present ills.

We are told that a thousand million people will be viewing the Royal Wedding on Television. It cannot be expected that a large proportion of them will be able to sing those words and give to them a great depth of meaning and sincerity. Yet I think, at this particular time, even a small proportion, making of them an act of re-dedication, would not be insignificant — if it were a re-dedication to that "sacrificial love" Spring-Rice had in mind, and if in our day we had in mind the building of a multi-racial society in our country of equal opportunities and mutual tolerance, in a country committed to serve the commonwealth of the world.

Given that interpretation — and it is an all-important proviso — I do not myself underestimate the power of those words:

I vow to thee my country — all earthly things above —
Entire and whole and perfect, the service of my love —
The love that asks no question; the love that stands the test,
That lays upon the altar the dearest and the best;
The love that never falters, the love that pays the price,
The love that makes undaunted the final sacrifice.

And Spring-Rice's death, so immediately after penning the final version of the second verse, can remind us of that other-worldly dimension which needs to be part of all our strivings in this world. It can remind us of the true context of our life and actions in this world.

And there's another country, I've heard of long ago —
Most dear to them that love her, most great to them that know.
We may not count her armies; we may not see her King;
Her fortress is a faithful heart, her pride is suffering;
And soul by soul and silently, her shining bounds increase,
And her ways are ways of gentleness and all her paths are peace.

THE FALKLANDS CRISIS

Gray's Inn Chapel: April 25th 1982

A phrase from this morning's Collect: "Guide with thy pure and peaceable wisdom those who take counsel for the nations of the earth".

I imagine you'll agree that we're bound to think together today about aspects of our Christian responsibility in the present crisis. My own thinking has been very considerably shaped by two quite different memories.

It so happens I was present in the gallery of the House of Commons, twenty years ago, when the Prime Minister, Harold Macmillan, described what the week of that crisis had felt like to him, when it was suddenly reported that Russia had built up a supply of nuclear missiles and launching sites in Cuba, and that a dozen more missile-carrying ships were on the way. In terms of stress, he said, it was the most horrible and distasteful week he could remember, in peace or war. All that week it had looked as though the world was on the brink of catastrophe; and he described how the pressures built up, on both sides, in public and private. He told us he was on the 'phone to the President of the United States, President Kennedy, as many as three times a day, often in the early hours.

The United States decided then, as we have done now, to do all it could to put a stop to the arms build-up with a blockade, a "quarantine", as it was called then. A miscalculation of what either side might do could have led to disaster. "We had to look into the cannon's mouth", the Prime Minister said, "without flinching". He went on to tell how the United States planned to invade Cuba at the end of the first week if the Russians didn't climb down. The possibility was considered — and rejected — of an immediate air strike to knock out the missiles and their bases. In that Cuba crisis there was, as there is now, the question of the part the United Nations might play: doing the independent inspecting work to see whether promises had been kept; guaranteeing this; supervising that; working out what bargaining there might be — if any. The question of trust was important and painfully difficult, since Mr Kruschev had at first lied about the very existence of the missiles and their bases.

What seemed unthinkable was that either side would — or could — give in. "Great powers do not give in", said Harold Macmillan, "not unless they have some way of saving their faces"; and it was difficult to see how there could be any face-saving in that situation. Yet, he said, it was important to try and provide some means of just that, if peace was to prevail. And then, to most people's astonishment, the Russians suddenly called their ships back, and dismantled the missile bases.

I reflect on that particular memory now because I don't think anything in these last twenty years has more informed the kind of prayers I believe we need to make about such situations, which seem to recur now with alarming regularity, around the globe.

Obviously there's the prayer for judgment and wisdom to be given to those who negotiate under such huge stress. There's the need of courage, but not the kind that pays no regard to what will help each side to make peace. There's the ability to listen, be sensitive and imaginative. Health obviously plays a significant part in long hours of negotiation under stress. And trust there has to be — at some stage; but trust has painfully to be re-established.

I personally think it doesn't take human sinfulness seriously enough just to ignore the role of power, the creative and redemptive use of power, in such negotiations.

But our heartfelt prayer has also to be for politicians who themselves have been or may yet be humiliated, to be delivered from intransigence and inflexibility and from a too narrow and face-saving patriotism that can be "trigger-happy" — in days when "trigger-happy" people, under the guise perhaps of defence of principles, can too easily and too quickly move their fingers not only to the triggers of conventional arms, but from there to the trigger of the missile. (And I suppose our supply of arms to Argentina up to the very last moment has already been one of the cautionary tales of the present situation.)

In fact, I sat in the gallery of the Commons that day, twenty years ago, with someone who is now the widow of one whose Memorial Service I attended, as some of you will no doubt have done, a little over a fortnight ago, in Westminster Abbey. Lady Butler was the mother of an undergraduate, now Vicar of St. Paul's, Knightsbridge, to whom I had been Chaplain at Cambridge. And the second memory which has shaped my thoughts on the crisis of the last few weeks is the memory of that Memorial Service to Lord Butler.

The Service was unforgettable, not least because of the events that had immediately preceded it. Lord Carrington had resigned as Foreign Secretary only an hour before the Service; but his first public duty after his resignation was to read a Lesson at that Service, before Prince Charles, the Prime Minister, four former British Prime Ministers, and a huge concourse of people from Parliament, the Diplomatic Service, and every walk of life in which Lord Butler had served.

But it was the words of the Lesson Lord Carrington had to read which gripped our attention. They were as poignant and dramatic as any Lesson which could have been chosen at that sombre hour: from the book of Wisdom, the Sixth Chapter, beginning at the 12th Verse, with those superb words:

> Wisdom is glorious and never fadeth away: yea, she is easily seen of them that love her, and found of such as seek her.

As Lord Carrington read that Lesson, with everyone's sympathy at having to read such a Lesson at such a time, he gradually made me feel that it was in fact as appropriate a Lesson for these times as anyone could choose. That day — that morning — the naval task force had set sail for the South Atlantic. Momentous decisions lay ahead for the new Foreign Secretary, for the Prime Minister, for Parliament, for those in command of the Naval Operation, for those who would negotiate on our behalf, and for the leaders of Argentina, indeed for us all.

I could imagine Lord Butler, who was as familiar as any with the complexity and responsibility of such decisions, being quietly pleased that such a Lesson had been selected for his Memorial Service, and at such a time, to fix our thoughts on the need above all for Wisdom.

The Archbishop of Canterbury summed up those thoughts in that most beautiful prayer of Francis Paget, former Bishop of Oxford: "Almighty God, from whom all thoughts of truth and peace proceed: Kindle we pray thee in the hearts of all men the true love of peace; and guide with thy pure and peaceable wisdom those who take counsel for the nations of the earth . . ."

But where does wisdom lead us, as Christians, in this particular situation? And is it "easily seen of them that love her"?

You may have seen *The Times* leading article yesterday which suggested that there were two possible Christian stances in relation to the crisis: the one, that of the total pacifist; and the other based on the doctrine of the "just" or "justifiable" War. In the name of love, reluctantly, sadly, Christians are sometimes compelled to use force, to repel aggression. But there can only be a "just" war if it is caused by injustice: if it resolutely aims to restore justice, and as resolutely to reach a better peace. And such a war must be conducted with the minimum force. A force dare not be used and a slaughter caused that is out of all proportion to the injustice done.

It would of course be simpler for us if we could immediately say that all the justice is on the British side and all the injustice on the side of Argentina. But one of my friends is the Bishop of Argentina, Richard Cutts, a British citizen in Argentina, a cool, quiet, rational person who firmly believes that the history of the Falklands in the last 150 years and in particular the last twenty years, justifies much of the Argentine's bitter sense of injustice, which we, concentrating simply on words like "sovereignty" or on the Argentine invasion of the Falklands itself — he maintains — tend to ignore. (Our own recent refusal of *full* British citizenship to the Falkland islanders itself queries the question of sovereignty.)

In our wisdom can we really envisage, I wonder, what is a minimum and "appropriate" use of force? Or that a military solution will in the long run serve the best interests of the surviving Falkland islanders? Can we be sure that minimum force will stop there and not escalate into a holocaust? Can force of arms, whichever way the battle goes, prove more than Might is Right — but leave the long term issues unresolved?

Or is there some imaginative, creative, yet wise act, with doubtless some sacrifice required from each party, which can yet persuade the Argentine Government to withdraw their forces, without losing too much face; which will prevent needless human slaughter, a vast and continuing expenditure on arms, and serve the best interests of all parties, and bring this sorry affair to a speedy end?

Today, at this late hour, we have not much time left to go on praying for wisdom. But that today we must surely do:

> Guide with thy pure and peaceable wisdom those who take counsel for the nations of the earth.

KIPLING AND REMEMBRANCE

Gray's Inn Chapel: November 14th 1982

There was a time when no Armistice Service was complete without Kipling's "Recessional"; but for many, Kipling epitomised the Empire, so when the Empire went, Kipling went. It followed that when *Hymns Ancient and Modern* was revised, the "Recessional" was sunk without trace.

Yet I myself think there are few better guides for our thoughts at Armistice-tide than Kipling; and especially so this Armistice, which follows the Battle for the Falklands.

There is always in Kipling, for good and ill, what I can only call a fundamentally "God-fearing" attitude. His poems are steeped in the Bible: from the Creation to the Last Great Bugle Call. Sometimes he speaks like a prophet of old, as in "Gehazi", which with savage and passionate invective cuts at Rufus Isaacs, who, after being implicated in the Marconi scandal, had become Lord Chief Justice. "The Road to Endor" is his equally bitter warning to war widows against the perils of spiritualism. But I don't myself think there are many poems of the Great War that portray more powerfully the horror of war than Kipling's "Gethsemane":

> The Garden called Gethsemane
>   In Picardy it was,
> And there the people came to see
>   The English soldiers pass.
> We used to pass — we used to pass
>   Or halt, as it might be,
> And ship our masks in case of gas
>   Beyond Gethsemane.

The Garden called Gethsemane,
  It held a pretty lass,
But all the time she talked to me
  I prayed my cup might pass.
The officer sat on the chair,
  The men lay on the grass,
And all the time we halted there
  I prayed my cup might pass.

It didn't pass — it didn't pass —
  It didn't pass from me.
I drank it when we met the gas
  Beyond Gethsemane!

Kipling has a fine Old Testament sense not only of the Creator God, but of a God who has given us our part to play in the world. The much loved "Sussex" he wrote in 1902 makes that as plain as it could be:

God gave all men all earth to love
  But, since our hearts are small,
Ordained for each one spot should prove.
  Belovèd over all;
That, as He watched Creation's birth,
  So we, in godlike mood,
May of our love create our earth
  And see that it is good.

Kipling has an Old Testament sense of the sanctity of the Law; of the purpose of God for mankind; of the balance that can only be restored by punishment or sacrifice; a sense of humanity somehow knitted into a great Family: a People — and of the presence of a righteous anger, a God of Judgment, at the heart of things, and at the end of things.

Those who know his great line in "The Ballad of East and West":

Oh, East is East, and West is West, and never the twain shall meet

often forget the second half of the phrase: that they *shall* meet when

*Earth and Sky stand presently at
God's great Judgment Seat.*

"Tomlinson" is taught at "Peter's Gate" about individual responsibility:

The sin ye do by two and two
  ye must pay for one by one.

But he is also taught about the necessity of finding a personal faith,

73

a personal relationship with God. There's no great value in

The God that you took from a printed book . . .

When I was a ten year old choirboy I remember singing an anthem, the words of which Kipling had written late in his life for the Pageant of Parliament in 1934. The words often come back to me, and I still think they say something worth saying:

Non nobis Domine! —
Not unto us, O Lord!
The Praise or Glory be
Of any deed or word;
For in Thy Judgment lies
To crown or bring to nought
All knowledge or device
That Man has reached or wrought.
And we confess our blame —
How all too high we hold
That noise which men call Fame,
That dross which men call Gold.
For these we undergo
Our hot and godless days,
But in our hearts we know
Not unto us the Praise.

And the last verse reveals that Kipling's picture of God has developed and grown over the years:

O Power by whom we live —
Creator, Judge, and Friend,
Upholdingly forgive
Nor fail us at the end:
But grant us well to see
In all our piteous ways
Non nobis Domine! —
Not unto us the Praise!

Kipling is able to put into simple words a simple yet strong faith. On Armistice Day there are many who want, for instance, to hear, and to believe, his line in "The Sack of the Gods":

He never wasted a leaf on a tree. Do you think He would squander souls?

Even before the War, Kipling's musings had led him towards the great theme of Redemption. In his poem, "The Rabbi's Song", he writes:

Our lives, our tears, as water,
Are spilled upon the ground;
God giveth no man quarter,

> Yet God a means hath found,
> Though Faith and Hope have vanished,
> And even Love grows dim —
> A means whereby His banished
> Be not expelled from Him!

But it was when his own son was killed in the war at the Battle of Loos in 1915, that, understandably, Kipling's deepest thoughts were revealed. I know of few more poignant poems in all English literature than one called "A Nativity 1914-1918" that was obviously written with his own son's death in mind:

> *The Babe was laid in the Manger*
> *Between the gentle kine —*
> *All safe from cold and danger —*
> 'But it was not so with mine,
>   (With mine! With mine!)
> 'Is it well with the child, is it well?'
>   The waiting mother prayed.
> 'For I know not how he fell,
>   And I know not where he is laid.'
>
> *A Star stood forth in Heaven;*
> *The Watchers ran to see*
> *The Sign of the Promise given*
>   'But there comes no sign to me.
>   (To me! To me!)
> '*My* child died in the dark.
>   Is it well with the child, is it well?
> There was none to tend him or mark,
>   And I know not how he fell.'
>
> *The Cross was raised on high;*
> *The Mother grieved beside —*
> 'But the Mother saw Him die
>   And took Him when He died.'
>   (He died! He died!)
>
> 'Seemly and undefiled
>   His burial-place was made —
> Is it well, is it well with the child?
>   For I know not where he is laid.'
>
> *On the dawning of Easter Day*
> *Comes Mary Magdalene;*
> *But the Stone was rolled away,*
>   *And the Body was not within —*
>   (Within! Within!)

'Ah, who will answer my word?'
   The broken mother prayed.
'They have taken away my Lord,
   And I know not where He is laid.'

'The Star stands forth in Heaven.
   The watchers watch in vain
For Sign of the Promise given
   Of peace on Earth again —
      (Again! Again!)

'But I know for Whom he fell' —
   The steadfast mother smiled,
'Is it well with the child — is it well?
   It is well — it is well with the child!'

T.S. Eliot, in his Introduction to his*"A Choice of Kipling's Verse"* reminds us that few men can make the most of such very different forms of expression as poetry and prose. Yet Kipling was, of course, as much a story teller as a poet. And most of his best poems are, in fact, stories. There is one remarkable story which has coupled to it a no less remarkable poem.

"The Gardener" is the story of a spinster who has brought up an illegitimate son as her dead brother's child. He was killed in the war. And going to visit his grave, burdened with the secret of her shame, she meets among the serried ranks of naked black crosses a figure who can only be the risen Christ. He answers her request to be shown her nephew's grave with the words, "Come with me and I will show you where your son lies". She goes away "supposing him to be the gardener". The woman's suffering, her son's death, God's Son's death and rising, bring her to an experience of "True Resurrection".

One of the reasons why I believe Kipling needs to be read today is because his travels had taught him what untravelled — and, often, much travelled — men and women of the Empire had not often learnt: to be appreciative of the religious experience of others and to be respectful of other faiths. It is only those who have not read Kipling who can accuse him of racial superiority. Indeed, another reason why Kipling needs to be read is his humour, his divinely inspired humour, not least on subjects of tension and conflict such as the one we now label "racism" — witness his poem "We and They":

Father, Mother, and Me,
   Sister and Auntie say
All the people like us are We,
   And every one else is They.

And They live over the sea,
    While We live over the way,
But — would you believe it? — They look upon We
    As only a sort of They!

We eat pork and beef
    With cow-horn-handled knives,
They who gobble Their rice off a leaf,
    Are horrified out of Their lives;
While They who live up a tree,
    And feast on grubs and clay,
(Isn't it scandalous?) look upon We
    As a simply disgusting They!

We shoot birds with a gun.
    They stick lions with spears.
Their full-dress is un-.
    We dress up to Our ears.
They like Their friends for tea.
    We like Our friends to stay;
And, after all that, They look upon We
    As an utterly ignorant They!

We eat kitcheny food.
    We have doors that latch.
They drink milk or blood,
    Under an open thatch.

We have Doctors to fee.
    They have Wizards to pay.
And (impudent heathen!) They look upon We
    As a quite impossible They!

All good people agree,
    And all good people say,
All nice people, like Us, are We
    And every one else is They:
But if you cross over the sea,
    Instead of over the way,
You may end by (think of it!) looking on We
    As only a sort of They!

There is no trace of *odium theologicum* in Kipling. "Look, you
have cast out Love!" is a powerful first line of a verse that in its last
refers to "cold Christ and tangled Trinities".

Kipling wrote characteristically in a letter: "I expect that every
man has to work out his creed according to his own wave-length, and

the hope is that the Great Receiving Station is tuned to take all wave-lengths.

One of his last poems, "Hymn of Breaking Strain", written in 1935, ends with the words:

Oh veiled and secret Power
  Whose paths we seek in vain,
Be with us in our hour
  Of overthrow and pain;
That we — by which sure token
  We know Thy ways are true —
In spite of being broken,
  Because of being broken
  May rise and build anew.
  Stand up and build anew!

And there I think I should end. And if only our hymn book included it, we should now rise and sing Kipling's "Recessional"; but, as I've said, when *Ancient and Modern* was revised, Kipling's "Recessional" was unceremoniously ditched. So I shall end — this Armistice, after the Falklands — by simply reading those lines that Kipling wrote in 1897 for Victoria's Diamond Jubilee, which have, I think, a curious power and eloquence this particular year of the Battle for the Falklands:

God of our fathers, known of old,
  Lord of our far-flung battle-line,
Beneath whose awful Hand we hold
  Dominion over palm and pine —
Lord God of Hosts, be with us yet,
Lest we forget — lest we forget!

The tumult and the shouting dies;
  The Captains and the Kings depart:
Still stands Thine ancient sacrifice,
  An humble and a contrite heart.
Lord God of Hosts, be with us yet,
Lest we forget — lest we forget!

Far-called, our navies melt away;
  On dune and headland sinks the fire:
Lo, all our pomp of yesterday
  Is one with Nineveh and Tyre!
Judge of the Nations, spare us yet.
Lest we forget — lest we forget!

If, drunk with sight of power, we loose
  Wild tongues that have not Thee in awe,
Such boastings as the Gentiles use,
  Or lesser breeds without the Law —
Lord God of Hosts, be with us yet,
Lest we forget — lest we forget!

For heathen heart that puts her trust
  In reeking tube and iron shard,
All valiant dust that builds on dust,
  And guarding, calls not Thee to guard,
For frantic boast and foolish word —
Thy mercy on Thy People, Lord!

THE PREACHER'S TASK
Gray's Inn Chapel: January 30th 1983

If I said, "The Archdeacon described him as 'the most thoroughly bestial creature that he had ever set eyes on' ", I have no doubt that you would immediately recognise that it was Mr. Slope, the Bishop of Barchester's Chaplain, to whom the Archdeacon was referring. You may even have remembered what pardonably occasioned the words: Mr. Slope's never-to-be-forgotten first sermon in the Cathedral at Barchester. But, unless you are an avid reader — as well as viewer — of Trollope, you may not remember his words by way of comment on that sermon:

> "There is" he says, "perhaps no greater hardship at present inflicted on mankind in civilised and free countries than the necessity of listening to sermons. No one but a preaching clergyman has, in these realms, the power of compelling an audience to sit silent, and be tormented. No one but a preaching clergyman can revel in platitudes, truisms, and *un*truisms, and yet receive, as his undisputed privilege, the same respectful demeanour as though words of impassioned eloquence, or persuasive logic, fell from his lips . . .
>
> Let a barrister attempt to talk without talking well, and he will talk but seldom. A judge's charge need be listened to perforce by none but the jury, prisoner, and gaoler . . . But no one can rid himself of the preaching clergyman . . We are not forced into church! No; but we desire more than that. We desire not to be forced to stay away. We desire, nay, we are resolute, to enjoy the comfort of public worship; but we desire also that we may do so without an amount of tedium which ordinary human nature cannot endure with patience; that we may be able to leave the house of God without that anxious longing for escape, which is the common consequence of common sermons."

After reading those chastening words for a Preacher — as I did, a few weeks ago, after reading *Barchester Towers* again, after seeing one or two episodes of the TV serial — I fell to thinking about preaching in a way I haven't thought about it for quite a while.

My parents were Non-conformists, so I was brought up with a high ideal of and regard for preaching. They would tell me of the great preachers they had heard at the turn of the century at, for instance, the City Temple: people like Dr. R. J. Campbell and Dr. Maude Royden. And I can myself remember so well the beginnings of broadcast sermons: by Canon W.H. Elliott from St. Michael's Chester Square, and Dick Sheppard and Pat McCormack from St. Martin-in-the-Fields. But I was dimly aware that the radio was in some way the death-knell of preaching. John Donne at St. Paul's and Lancelot Andrewes, of this Ancient and Honourable Society, would go on for hours; but the BBC ask you to keep it to four minutes!

I noticed we had only a two minute slice of Slope on television, and that was quite enough!

The demise of preaching is, of course, part of the decay, or at least the change, in so much else: the drift away from organised religion; the changing patterns of worship; the dialogue, the panel and the shared discussion, taken as inevitably having a greater breadth of awareness and depth of truth than the monologue; the significance of "eye-gate" as well as "ear-gate" in a televisual age, which makes the dance, the mime and the drama of such huge cultural importance; a clergy whose numbers are dwindling, helplessly caught up in all sorts of priorities which seem to rate higher than the preparation of a sermon; the decline, or at least the suspicion, of oratory and the orator; the change of attitude towards all who claim to speak with authority. And I have to say quite frankly that I am thankful I am usually too busy preaching to have to listen to many sermons. And why shouldn't I say that if I go to church on holiday I go with an awful fear that I shall be bored, and that that fear is quite often fulfilled? Or, if I'm not bored, I so disagree with the picture of God that I'm given, by some over-simplifying or superficial evangelist, that I come out fretful rather than at peace. And, of course, Biblical scholarship is a huge contributory factor in what I will call the undermining of preaching. Nineteenth century preachers used with confidence to expatiate upon the details of the life of Jesus. Now we know the birth narratives, for instance, are not to be trusted for their historicity; and that each evangelist had his own axe to grind when he said what he believed Jesus had said. Indeed, it's not easy to say now that Jesus actually said this or that, or to distinguish what he said from what those-who-said-that-he-said-this-or-that said! Why then, you may ask, are you Preacher to Gray's Inn — and, what's more, seem — for the most part — to enjoy it?

The answer to that is strangely simple. I believe that, in spite of all the difficulties, what as Preacher I have to point towards is of the utmost importance. And, in the end, that is not primarily a matter of say, skill with words. What a preacher has to do, I believe, is to point toward a Mystery, not to teach a system of thought and then demonstrate that nothing can disturb it. I have to point, again and again, in this way and that, to the Mystery of God's love at the very heart of the universe.

Baron Von Hügel wrote: "Never get things too clear. Religion can't be clear. In this mixed up life there is always an element of unclearness . . . If I could understand religion as I understand that two and two make four, it would not be worth understanding. Religion can't be clear if it's worth having. To me, if I can see things through, I get uneasy. I feel it's a fake. I know I have left something out. I've made some mistake."

I think a preacher, like a poet, ought to be aware that he can never say *exactly* what he means. Yet he must try as best he can to say that the Mystery of the Love of God is the one thing that's fundamental; and he must say it, as Jesus did, by talking of everyday things and God at the heart of them: things maybe that people are involved in at the time, or will be; and he must remember that for all of us, whoever we are, some of the most certain facts of life are suffering and death.

I think sermons should help people understand themselves better, should help people understand who they are more profoundly, because the Kingdom of Heaven is within each one of us.

Of course it takes an extraordinary courage and grace to face the Mystery of who we are, so I suppose a preacher's task is in part to encourage and help people, if he can, to face that Mystery.

What Dame Helen Gardner writes of the Art of T.S. Eliot has, I think, much to say about preaching. "It is not the poet's business", she writes, "to make us believe *what* he believes, but to make us believe *that* he believes. He must convince us that what he believes genuinely interprets, makes sense of, experience which we recognise as our own. Although we may not accept his interpretation, we must feel it is a real interpretation."

A "real interpretation". That's what I think a sermon should be. My favourite alternative word for a preacher is simply an "interpreter". Even that is perhaps a little too confident if you think of it as someone who can easily be didactic, over dogmatic in his interpreting.

A preacher is like someone who holds a sea shell to his ear and then has to try to say what he's heard. And he knows that he's very privileged to have heard what he's heard, and as privileged to be called to interpret it.

Interpreting the Mystery of Love. You wouldn't have known that was the role of Mr. Slope that memorable morning in Barchester. But neither would you have guessed that Christ was love that day he cleansed the Temple with a whip of small cords in his hands, the sweat pouring off his face.

So it's not only tender shepherds who reveal the Mystery of Love. The prophets do so as well. And prophecy and preaching are near neighbours. Perhaps the greatest preacher of our time has been Martin Luther King, whose sermons were published under the title *Strength to Love*. But you will remember, Martin Luther King was assassinated for what he preached — because he had the strength to say that the Mystery of Love and the cause of Negro Civil Rights are inseparable.

Yet Martin Luther King's last sermon said something about the Mystery of Love: that it is always greater than the preacher's words or vision: it is greater than this world.

He said — significantly, as I say, in his last sermon, just before he was assassinated:

I don't know what will happen now.
We've got some difficult days ahead.
But it doesn't matter to me now.
Because I've been to the mountain top, I won't mind.
Like anybody else, I would like to live a long life.
Longevity has its place.
But I'm not concerned about that now.
I just want to do God's will.
And He's allowed me to go up to the mountain top.
And I've looked over, and I've seen the Promised Land.
So, I'm happy tonight. I'm not worried about anything.
I'm not fearing any man. Mine eyes have seen the glory
of the coming of the Lord . . .

He had seen the Mystery of Love, and was interpreting it in terms of the realities of his surrounding world and society.

GANDHI
Gray's Inn Chapel: April 24th 1983

I have only to say to you "Eight Oscars", and you will know immediately what is to be the centre of my sermon.

But what precisely should I say in a sermon — in Gray's Inn — about the film of *Gandhi*?

There are to my mind several "messages", so to speak, in the film that we could profitably consider in Chapel.

There's the unforgettable scene near the film's end when a Hindu from the slums, both a victim of and a perpetrator of violence, comes face to face with Gandhi. In revenge for the death of his own son at Moslem hands, the Hindu has killed a Moslem boy. "I am going to Hell," he says — and looks as though he's already there. Gandhi, on a cot, and nearly dead from a fast, looks at the young Hindu, and says: "I know a way out of Hell. Find a child whose parents have been killed in the riots, and love the child as your own. But let it be a *Moslem* orphan, and raise the child as a Moslem."

On another occasion, confronted with an anti-Moslem crowd of Hindus, Ben Kingsley's Gandhi tells them: "I am a Moslem — and a Hindu and a Christian and a Jew. For God's sake, let us embrace one another like brothers."

The gradual change in Gandhi over the years is worth our reflecting upon here in Chapel: his increasing indentification with and commitment to the poor, signified in his clothing. At first, in the film, he is a well-dressed young lawyer, travelling in a first-class compartment in South Africa. Later, in India, he wears nothing more than a loin cloth. Thereby he reminds the wealthy, wherever they come from, of the dignity of the poor. In his personal renunciation of wealth for a life of simplicity, the film reminds us that in many ways Gandhi was a modern St. Francis, speaking to rich and poor alike of the joy of travelling light in this world.

That beginning of the film in South Africa has something else to say to us. The well-dressed young Indian barrister is literally thrown out of the first-class compartment on to the platform at Pietermaritzburg, exposing to South African audiences certainly — but not to them alone — the evils of apartheid, for what they were and what they still are, and reminding us that apartheid has changed, but has not changed all that much in a century, so that the number of lawyers raised up from within the vast South African black community has been tragically few.

All these scenes have something for our reflection here in Chapel.

Yet there is one scene which I think we should particularly ponder here in some detail, for reasons which I hope will become plain.

It's a hot March day in Ahmedebad in 1922. Gandhi is being tried before Mr. Robert Broomfield of the Indian Civil Service, District and Sessions Judge. Sir J.P. Strangman, the Advocate-General, states the case for the prosecution, saying that the charge is that of bringing, or attempting to bring, into hatred or contempt, His Majesty's Government, established by law in British India, and that Gandhi is guilty because of three articles he has written and published in his weekly magazine, *Young India*.

Gandhi pleads guilty to all the charges.

The Advocate-General then goes on to say that Gandhi is a man of high educational qualifications, and, evidently from his writings, a recognised leader; and the court must consider to what the results of a campaign of the nature disclosed in his writings must inevitably lead. In the preceding three months, there had been riots in Bombay on the occasion of the arrival of the Prince of Wales, when a large number of persons were killed and wounded; and at Chauri Chaura, when a mob, fired on by the police, got out of control and set fire to the police station, killing twenty-two policemen. Gandhi, says the Advocate-General, in his articles preached non-violence. But what was the use of preaching non-violence when he preached dissatisfaction towards the Government or openly instigated others to overthrow it?

The judge, who, significantly, when he takes his seat, bows to his distinguished prisoner, asks Gandhi whether he wishes to make a statement. Gandhi says he does, but adds:

"Before I read my statement, I would like to state that the learned Advocate-General was entirely fair to me in all the statements he has made, and I have no desire to conceal from this court the fact that to preach disaffection toward the existing system of government has become almost a passion with me. And in the statement that I am about to read, it will be my painful duty to admit before this court that it commenced much earlier than the period stated by the Advocate-General. It is the most painful duty for me, but I have to discharge that duty knowing the responsibility that rests on my shoulders in connection with the Bombay occurrences and the Chauri Chaura occurrences. Thinking over these deeply, and sleeping over them night after night, it is impossible for me to dissociate myself from the diabolical crimes of Chauri Chaura or the mad outrages of Bombay. He is quite right when he says that as a man of responsibility, a man having received a fair share of education, having had a fair share of experience of this world, I should have known the consequences of every one of my acts. I knew that I was playing with fire. I ran the risk, and if I was set free I would still do the same. I have felt this morning that I would have failed in my duty if I did not say this."

"I wanted to avoid violence," Gandhi goes on. "Non-violence is the first article of my creed . . . but I had to make my choice. I had either to submit to a system which I considered has done an irreparable harm to my country, or incur the risk of the mad fury of my people bursting forth, when they understood the truth from my lips. I know that my people have sometimes gone mad. I am deeply sorry for it, and I am therefore here to submit not to a light penalty but to the heaviest penalty. I do not ask for mercy. I do not plead any extenuating act. I am here, therefore, to invite and cheerfully submit to the highest penalty that can be inflicted upon me for what in law is a deliberate crime and what appears to me to be the highest duty of a citizen."

"The only course open to you, the judge," Gandhi says, "is either to resign your post, or inflict on me the severest penalty, if you believe that the system and law you are assisting to administer are good for the people. I do not expect that kind of conversion, but by the time I have finished with my statement, you will perhaps have a glimpse of what is raging within my breast and which has made me run this maddest of risks which a sane man can run."

Gandhi pauses, unfolds his statement, adjusts his steel-rimmed spectacles, looks about the room, filled with his followers, who sit still and motionless, and reads:

"I owe it perhaps to the Indian public, and to the public in England, to placate which this prosecution is mainly taken up, that I should explain why from a staunch loyalist and co-operator I have become an uncompromising disaffectionist and non-co-operator. To the court I should say why I plead guilty to the charge of promoting disaffection toward the government established by law in India."

Gandhi then gives virtually a potted history of his encounters with British authority — beginning as an Indian with few rights in South Africa. This speech is printed in full in *Gandhi: A Memoir* by William Shirer, who was present in court that day. The judge, Shirer records, seemed moved by Gandhi's words and said:

"Mr. Gandhi, you have made my task easy in one way by pleading guilty to the charge. Nevertheless, what remains, namely the determination of a just sentence, is perhaps as difficult a proposition as a judge in this country could have to face. The law is no respecter of persons. Nevertheless, it will be impossible to ignore the fact that you are in a different category from any person I have ever tried or am likely to try. It would be impossible to ignore the fact that in the eyes of millions of your countrymen you are a great patriot and a great leader. Even those who differ from you in politics look upon you as a man of high ideals and of a noble and even saintly life. I have to deal with you in one character only. It is not my duty and I do not presume to judge or criticise you in any other character. It is my duty to judge you as a man subject to the law, who by his own admission has broken the law and committed what to an ordinary man must appear to be a grave offence against the State.

"I do not forget that you have consistently preached against violence and that you have on many occasions, as I am willing to believe, done much to prevent violence. But having regard to the nature of your political teaching and the nature of many of those to whom it was addressed, how you could have continued to believe that violence would not be the inevitable consequence of it passes my capacity to understand.

"There are probably few people in India who do not sincerely regret that you should have made it impossible for any government to leave you at liberty. But it is so. I am trying to balance what is due to you against what appears to me to be necessary in the interest of the public, and I propose in passing sentence to follow the precedent of a case, in many respects similar to this case, that was decided some twelve years ago. The sentence then passed was of simple imprisonment for six years. You will not consider it unreasonable. And I should like to say in doing so that if the course of events in India makes it possible for the government to reduce the period and release you no one will be better pleased than I."

Gandhi, smiling at the sentence, said he simply wanted to add one word.

"So far as the sentence itself is concerned", he said, "I certainly consider it as light as any judge would inflict on me, and so far as the whole proceedings are concerned, I must say that I could not have expected greater courtesy."

As the judge left the bench, he bowed once more to the prisoner, who bowed in return.

I have recounted this strange, historic trial at length and in some detail for one reason only.

I saw the film and read the record of that trial the week that I was also having to read — and, indeed, prepare a broadcast comment upon for the World Service of the BBC — a Report that was put before the British Council of Churches at its Assembly last month, entitled *Civil Disobedience and Christian Obedience*. Gandhi's trial before Judge Broomfield caused me to think a very great deal about that subject.

87

I wonder what you think now — as Christians — of Gandhi's words, and, indeed, of his Civil Disobedience — in the light of history.

Few people in Western Europe question the use of passive resistance in, say, Poland or Afghanistan. But it is clear that the British with whom Gandhi had to deal were not a brutal tyranny, but were for the most part intelligent and sensitive men. When Gandhi confronted Judge Broomfield it was in many ways a case of two representatives of the same tradition, and, indeed, of the same profession, who respected each other because their values were shared. Nevertheless, *in conscience* Gandhi felt bound to say what he said and do and continue to do what he did. And the question the Churches in Britain are suddenly having to examine is whether non-violent civil disobedience in a democracy is ever to be supported and encouraged.

In his trial in South Africa recently, the Dutch Reformed pastor, Beyers Naudé, said: "The believer in Christ not only has the right but the responsibility to hearken to the Word of God and his righteousness rather than to the Government, should the Government deviate from God's Word. Civil Disobedience is an act of protest by the Christian on the grounds of Christian conscience. It is only permissible when authority expects of him an un-Christian deed, and pleas for return to observance of the Gospel have not availed . . . When the Government deviates from the Gospel," he said, "the Christian is bound by his conscience to resist it. Even if this results in breaking the law, it has to be done, because God's will must be maintained above the law of man."

However passionately Christians in Britain believe — as all of us, I am sure, here believe — that the law should be obeyed, and that where it is challenged, it should be done through constitutional and parliamentary means, it would be difficult — indeed, it is impossible — to maintain on theological grounds that there are *no* circumstances where civil disobedience is not permissible and right.

One might say that ever since Jesus suffered under Pontius Pilate, the subject of Civil Disobedience and Christian Obedience has, in fact, been with us; but now it is probably raising its head and its voice again.

I would end with only one more paragraph.

Mahatma Gandhi was, of course, a member of one of the Inns of Court of this great city. He was admitted to the Inner Temple on November 6th 1888. The way that Ancient and Honourable Society treated him — for good and ill — had, of course, lasting effect upon him. At the time he was just one more Overseas Student. But no one can read the writings and speeches of Gandhi and no one can observe his bearing — in, for instance, Ben Kingsley's remarkable portrayal of Gandhi — and not conclude that English Christianity and the English legal tradition played some considerable part in teaching Mohandas Karamchand Gandhi — and teaching him most splendidly — the love of that Justice which towers above even the best human laws.

THE HEREAFTER
Gray's Inn Chapel: November 6th 1983

The death of three members of the Inn this week, two of them on All Saints' Day, dictates what shall be the subject of my sermon.

But the form of it is dictated by the imminent death, humanly speaking, of a friend of mine, Bishop John Robinson, whom I met first over twenty-five years ago, when he was Dean of Clare College, Cambridge, and I was Chaplain of Trinity. He later became my Bishop, as Bishop of Woolwich, when we went together from Cambridge to South London. He eventually returned to Cambridge, to his present position as Dean of Trinity College; but last May he was told he had inoperable cancer and was given six months to live.

When John Robinson's *Honest to God* was published, twenty years ago, as many people felt liberated as were scandalised. Many in their hearts had never really believed in the God 'up there', or even 'out there'. It made sense for them to think of God in terms of the here and now: of God in the depth and ultimate significance of life and as the personification of moral and religious values. But the one aspect which would not fit easily into that scheme was belief in life-after-death. If the reality of God is interpreted, without remainder, into terms of present and personal values and experience, what becomes of a future hope beyond these terms? Wherein is it to be grounded?

It has to be admitted that belief in an after-life does not come naturally to many today. Even many theologians make heavy weather of it or leave it alone. Philosophers and novelists tend to take it for granted that death is total extinction. Ordinary folk, in spite of the current interest in the occult, seem to be little influenced by considerations of what might happen to them after death. Don Cupitt, the Dean of Emmanuel College, Cambridge, dismays me by stating as a Christian priest: "I do not claim that there is any supernatural being or realm of activity, nor that there is any part of us that will survive our deaths". I don't think that a Christian priest can be much more chilling than that.

But it's perhaps worth reminding ourselves that the Jews had no belief in personal life after death until very close to the time of Our Lord, and not all of them believed in it then.

The traditional God of Judaism today is the same as that of Christianity and Islam: one who promises a blessed immortality to those who love him, but not to all; whilst, of course, ideas of Nirvana, a state in which the individual is absorbed into some kind of impersonal Absolute, are found in the various forms of Buddhism.

Don Cupitt, in an intriguing sentence, speaks of the need we human beings have to "gain something of the never wasted integrity and completeness of a work of art. When lives are rounded off in that way", he says, "death loses its sting".

That sounds good, and there's undoubtedly a truth there. But it's a rather academic 'ivory tower' sort of statement. Birth, circumstances, upbringing and temperament, do give to some favoured souls a life that is 'rounded off' — on this earth.

But what about the others: the misfits, the crazed and possessed, the incurable depressives and schizophrenics, the victims of appalling tragedy or gross exploitation? What about the millions killed in the prime of their lives: the victims of man's inhumanity to man; the victims of grinding poverty; the many millions today whose malnutrition is such as to make life bereft of almost any value? In what sense can it be said that their lives are 'rounded off'?

Life, it seems to me, deals the cards so capriciously. Some are given a flying start and an abrupt end. Some from start to finish suffer appalling and crippling handicap.

It might be said that even tragic or premature death may, like all forms of suffering, be turned to good through faith and acceptance. I can see, for instance, that the parents of a young man with a promising future but killed by illness or accident, may through that tragic event themselves discover resources of faith and courage they never imagined they possessed. But what of the young man himself?

As a Christian, I find myself requiring of a God of Love — if he *be* a God of Love — something which cannot be supplied in and through this life alone.

Of course, this is dangerous ground. It can sound too much like the victims of sweated labour, who in Victorian times were advised to accept their lot, because, after death, there would be rest from their labours and reward for them. I even heard a bishop a short while ago say that "to the Christian the incineration of millions by a nuclear bomb is not the evil it might be to non-Christians; for we believe in Another World Than This".

But it is very dangerous to let Another World Than This take your eyes off this one.

I prefer the sentiments of that marvellous 18th Century hymn, "My God, I love thee, not because I hope for heaven thereby", which was even more marvellously translated from the Latin by Gerard Manley Hopkins:

O God, I love thee, I love thee —
Not out of hope of heaven for me
Nor fearing not to love and be
   In the everlasting burning.
Thou, thou, my Jesus, after me
   Didst reach thine arms out dying,
For my sake sufferedst nails and lance
Mocked and marrèd countenance,
   Sorrows passing number,
   Sweat and care and cumber,
Yea, and death, and this for me,
   And thou couldst see me sinning:
Then I, why should not I love thee,
Jesus, so much in love with me?
Not for heaven's sake; not to be
Out of hell by loving thee;
Not for any gains I see;
But just the way that thou didst me
I do love and I will love thee:
What must I love thee, Lord, for then?
For being my king and God. Amen.

The Church does not teach that the *motive* for the love of God is hope of heaven or fear of hell. And to me the reason for the after-life is not personal self-interest or the need for consolation, but the justification of God's dealings with mankind: the justification of the dealings in which He created man — the hungry infants in Ethiopia, for instance; the justification of the dealings in which he created the whole universe; the dealings in which he revealed His love for man, on the Cross, which are often so contradicted by things in this world alone. All these demand that this world should not be the end, that this life should not come to an abrupt end. Any other idea goes clean contrary to the idea that God will not lose "one of these little ones" who matter to him; that He will somehow "gather up the fragments, that nothing be lost". Of course, what form that after-life will take is another matter. That is up to Him: up to His Creative and Redeeming Love. And for me that is best expressed in the Prayer Book Collect for the Sixth Sunday after Trinity:

O GOD, who hast prepared for them that love thee such good things as pass man's understanding: Pour into our hearts such love toward Thee, that we, loving thee above all things, may obtain thy promises, which exceed all that we can desire; through Jesus Christ our Lord. Amen.

THE GOOD SHEPHERD TODAY

Gray's Inn Chapel: November 25th 1984

I have been told many a time that the parable of the Good Shepherd is too rural to be relevant to our urbanised society today. I can only say that in each stage of my adult life — as a teenager in my riverside wharf office; in two parishes; as chaplain of a Cambridge college; in two cathedral canonries; on two diocesan staff meetings; and now, running a charity; and not forgetting my task as Preacher here — I have found no passage of scripture *more* relevant and modern. It is to me as though Jesus had anticipated modern management consultancy, and got there first, so to speak, and set us all fundamental, unchanging and unchangeable questions.

"*I AM* the Good Shepherd".

"I AM" is, of course, a feature of St. John's Gospel. There are seven great declaratory sentences in St. John beginning "I AM". It is John declaring that Jesus is *the* "I AM": the Great Creator. It is John's way of saying what Matthew also said: "*All* authority is given unto me." "Yes" John seems to say "And all that authority is the power to *shepherd.*" — "I AM the Good Shepherd".

The first lesson from the parable is that wherever power and authority are concentrated, there is the opportunity and responsibility of shepherding.

Whether you are a McGregor or a Scargill; the Prime Minister or a Press Baron, an advertising agent, a teacher, or a parent; the Prince of Wales; the Treasurer of Gray's Inn, the Dean of Chapel, or the Preacher: authority is the power to shepherd.

"I am the Good Shepherd." Israel, Ezekiel reminds us, had some bad shepherds. But there is a hint in the parable of someone who is good at his job: an advertisement for shepherding, attractive. Before

94

the metaphor becomes a metaphor it speaks of someone who has something to contribute to the world by doing a down-to-earth job, and doing it well, and in so doing finds himself valuable and valued.

Visiting a Cheshire Home in Dulwich some years ago, I so well remember a paralysed young man basket-making in bed. He seemed to shepherd the few resources that remained to him, just out of an iron lung, and thus to rediscover his value. It is this which says something to us about shepherding, employment, and unemployment. There are various ways of keeping people off the human slag-heap, even when they're unemployed. Everyone has *some* capacity in them for shepherding. To be human is to be a pastor. We need to do all we can to keep that capacity alive in employed and unemployed, and to let that spur us to diminish the number of unemployed.

"He that is an hireling, whose own the sheep are not". A hireling is someone who's there for the hire, not for the sheep: not to do the job of shepherding. Strictly speaking, he's a sort of monetarist. He gives money the top priority.

I meet a good many people these days who thought they were valued in their firm till the take-over or the redundancy. But "when the crunch came", "when the chips were down" — there are many such phrases — they discovered they had been living with an illusion: the illusion that they mattered and were cared for, and were part of a flock and a fold and a family. And the discovery that they were *not* is the *really* bitter pill.

"Whose own" the sheep are not.

Hirelings are often made by management who fail in their shepherding: who treat the staff as though they were simply employees who get an income, and have no other value or contribution to the organisation.

Managers who are shepherds *prevent* hirelings.

"The hireling sees the wolf coming and leaves the sheep, and flees, and the wolf snatches them and scatters them . . ."

The wolf, the destroyer, takes many forms in this world. He can be dressed up, as in Red Riding Hood, in many deceptive garbs: as a policeman, a landlord, a boss, or even as an efficient administrator.

In this life the sheep are scattered most often, not killed. If they're not shepherded, they'll be scattered. They'll find somewhere: but they'll bear the teeth-marks of the wolf for quite a time, maybe for life. They may have a breakdown and be found in some clinic or hospital, or survive only on drugs and be labelled an addict, and have the guilt of the situation fixed entirely on them. They may be scattered to the street corners and get up to this and that. Maybe even to those in the highest positions of authority the guilt will simply be theirs: the sheep's, not the shepherd's.

The Good Shepherd doesn't just dismiss people. They're "his own". He can never give up the sheep. He can no more give them up than give up himself. They're part of himself. He can't simply "put them away".

The hireling "cares nothing for the sheep". Such a simple statement. But "don't care will be made to care", whether it's a don't care employer, organisation or country.

"I am the Good Shepherd: I know my own *and my own know Me.*"

"My own know me." That finishes once and for all authority on a pedestal. To allow oneself to be known means that what one *is* is all important: alongside people with our disguises off, enabling them to see who we really are and to trust us. It was said of Jesus: "This man receiveth sinners *and eateth with them!*" He let people know Him. That was how he exercised His authority. "My own know me." This essential reciprocity kills all paternalism; slaughters the know-all in us: the shepherd who thinks he knows exactly what's best for the silly sheep.

"The Good Shepherd giveth his life for the sheep."

Last Monday I spent six hours in Camberwell police station. It was a place that was all too familiar to me when I was a vicar in Camberwell twenty years ago, and I was very glad to go back there. To be honest, I've had some very negative experiences of the police in the last year; in parts of Liverpool, East London, and elsewhere; and I rather needed a good experience of the police. Thankfully, I was not disappointed. Indeed, I'd have to say that no matter how hard or deep I probed, I could only praise what I found. I saw how Community Policing and Neighbourhood Care work in an area with which I am fully familiar and which is by no means an easy area. Two social workers attached to the police station were looking after a huge case-load of families in which there is some kind of violence against children.

"The *Law* is my shepherd". Many children and many parents would be able to say that with some experience.

"The Law as *Shepherd*". There are over 400 magistrates for inner Manchester at the moment, but only a few of them live *within* the "urban priority areas". If the Law is to be understood it must be understood and experienced locally. There must be access to it. It must be seen to be shepherd and friend: as part of "us", not simply as "them". Law Centres seem to me to have a hugely important part to play in "the Law as Shepherd".

There was no incongruity in Israel in the concept of the Shepherd-King. Shepherds in Israel were rich and powerful. The

Woolsack today signifies how powerful shepherds once were even in Western Society. Power and riches bear with them the responsibility of shepherding. Shepherd Kings . . . Shepherd *Judges*?

We're told in the parable that the Good Shepherd "calleth his own sheep by name" — which, in Hebrew, means "by nature". ("Hallowed be thy Name", means "Hallowed be thy Nature".) But to know the sheeps' nature means to know what makes them tick: their qualities, their limitations, their circumstances, their habits — which means more than a kind of computerised knowledge. You have to be willing to spend time with people to know them in that sort of way.

"The sheep follow Him" — the Good Shepherd — "and a stranger will they not follow, but will flee from him: for they know not the voice of strangers".

We don't speak of "the voice of the stranger" these days. It's far too plain English! We prefer to speak of "the problem of communication". Alright! The sheep flee from "the non-communicator". The voice of the Good Shepherd they hear, and know, and recognise, and warm to.

When I came to Gray's Inn in 1978, several people said to me: "You're lucky to be going there. It's a very friendly Inn of Court." It's important surely, that the Law and Good Shepherding go together, and are seen to go together. It's important therefore that an Inn of Court is, and is seen to be, an example of Good Shepherding to all who in any way belong to it or serve it. And we dare not underestimate what is involved in the task of Good Shepherding. One Good Shepherd said it meant giving your life — which it did for Him.

We're told that when Jesus spake this parable unto them "they understood not what things he spake unto them." Part of me says: "They understood alright!" But the implications of the parable were too much for them: too costly. So the parable fell on deaf ears — which is always possible with parables . . . as it is with sermons.

THE ADORATION OF THE KINGS

Gray's Inn Chapel: January 20th 1985

At the National Gallery at the moment there's a remarkable exhibition, ostensibly for children. It's one entire room, devoted to only one painting, *The Adoration of the Kings*, by the early 16th Century Netherlandish artist, Gossaert — of whom, I fear, I'd never heard.

The exhibition is beautifully set out. The details of the painting have been photographed and enlarged, and the enlargements are set in different parts of the room; so that you can look separately at the Three Kings: Caspar (or Jasper), meaning "the white one", with his name on the lid of the chalice that carries his gift of gold. He has laid down his magnificent sceptre on the floor, in front of the new-born King. He himself kneels at the feet of the Virgin. The black King, Balthazar, meaning "Lord of the Treasures" — his name is on his crown — presents his gift of frankincense in an elaborate coffer, which is also clearly an example of the goldsmith's work of the times. Melchior — "King of Light" — has his own retinue, as do each of the Kings, as he comes to present his gift of myrrh. The aged Joseph watches from a doorway. So does the ox. The ass is more interested in his food. Some shepherds peep from behind piers. You can see their sheep in far away fields. Angels fill the sky. They carry a scroll with "Gloria" inscribed on it. A couple of Dürer-like dogs occupy the foreground. In the very centre of the painting, the Virgin sits with her Son on her lap, in a ruined temple rather than a stable.

High up on one of its capitals is a carving of Abraham offering up Isaac. Right at the top of the painting — again, in the centre — is the Star. You have no doubt it is meant to be God himself; and, just beneath the Star, hovers a dove.

It must be one of the most sumptuous versions of the subject ever painted. It was executed first, most probably, as an altar-piece. For brilliance of colour — the Virgin in glorious ultramarine — and for richness of detail, it must be one of the most ambitious works of those first years of the 16th Century.

Of course, there's more than one "Adoration of the Kings" in the National Gallery. I went and looked at one or two of them after looking at Gossaert's painting: one by Gerard David, Gossaert's contemporary; one, on wood, by the Venetian, Giorgione; one by Bruegel the Elder; and another by Botticelli. The same subject; but all incredibly different.

It's important, I think, to reflect on that fact; for those different interpretations speak of a process which had been going on from the beginning.

No one before Tertullian, in the 2nd Century, ever thought of those kings as *kings*. Up to then, they were astrologers from the Persian Court. In the wall paintings of the catacombs and in some Byzantine mosaics they wear Mithraic robes. No one actually named them until the 9th Century. Their names first appear in a Ravenna pontifical (or episcopal prayerbook): the same names as appear six centuries later in Gossaert's painting. Gradually the three Kings come to personify the three parts of the known world: Europe, Africa, Asia.

The Venerable Bede, in the 7th Century, gives each of the gifts a symbolic meaning: gold, homage to Christ's kingship; frankincense, homage to his divinity; myrrh, foreshadowing his embalming and death.

I said that that process had been going on from the beginning, because, for instance, there aren't three wise men in St. Matthew's record — the only biblical record; there are three gifts; but it's possible for, say, one Father Christmas to carry three or thirty-three gifts, and it would be disastrous if at the check-out at Sainsbury's one person could only carry one purchase.

St. Matthew's story is of course his own contribution to the interpretative process. It's very clearly Matthew's painting, his illustration, in legendary form, of Old Testament themes — "The Kings of Tharsis and of the Isles shall give presents: the Kings of Arabia and Saba shall bring gifts . . ." And "Gentiles shall come to thy light, and kings to the brightness of thy rising."

Most Biblical scholars see Matthew doing just what Gossaert did: using the materials that were to hand in his day, that were natural to him; using his gifts to portray the truth as he saw it.

No one can survey what artists of one kind and another have done with this story down the ages: in music — like that lovely carol of Peter Cornelius: "Three Kings from Persian Lands Afar"; in painting;

in poetry — like Eliot's "Journey of the Magi": no one can survey all this artistic creation and not recognise that here is a tale of mystery and imagination that has huge power to stimulate the heart and mind and the creative imagination. This story of all stories, this incident of all incidents, brings us all, whoever we are, to the gates of adoration, of worship, and of response to God.

W.H. Auden, in his poem, "For the Time Being", puts into the mouth of the first Wise Man the words:

> To discover how to be truthful now
> Is the reason I follow this star.

The second Wise Man says:

> To discover how to be living now
> Is the reason I follow this star.

And the third:

> To discover how to be loving now
> Is the reason I follow this star.

And then, together, they say:

> To discover how to be human now
> Is the reason we follow this star.

It's easy nevertheless to be simply an onlooker at the Epiphany: to read St. Matthew's story much as I gazed at Gossaert's painting. But there's a second stage when we let the story make us part of it. That is what Matthew and Gossaert and many another have done.

If we were in school, and if I were a teacher, at this point, I would probably say: "Now for your homework I want you to express in any medium you like what the story means for you." We might surprise one another at what we produced!

If you paint, I wonder what you would do today, for instance, with the Black Balthazar? An Ethiopian Wise Man has a tragic as well as a topical ring this year.

I've recently been reading the *Report of the Race Relations Committee of the Senate of the Inns of Court and of the Bar*. It has made me wonder whether to make Balthazar contemporary — as contemporary as Gossaert made him — he should perhaps be painted as a black barrister. "Able black barristers", I gather from the Report, "find it extremely difficult to get a tenancy in an established white set of chambers". Certainly I would have to paint him at the moment as one of those regal black young men whom you see so often at street corners in, say, Lambeth or Notting Hill: who have so many gifts, but whose gifts so often remain unused. I can even hear a snatch of the conversation at the manger: "I've brought these gifts to You.

I knew *You'd* value them. My sort of gifts seem not to be needed in England just now." Though one in twenty of the population of Britain are black, less than one in a hundred of the police force are. The legal profession have an equally poor record.

The habit of interpreting eternal truths by clothing them in the dress, the language and the culture of the contemporary world can be as beautiful as Gossaert's work. It can at the same time be disturbing, challenging, painful, even frightening.

Yet the last word of the Epiphany story must always, I think, be one of hope, indeed of joy.

Auden ends his "Oratorio", as he calls the long poem from which I have already quoted, with these words:

He is the Way.
Follow Him through the land of Unlikeness;
You will see rare beasts, and have unique adventures.

He is the Truth.
Seek Him in the Kingdom of Anxiety;
You will come to a great city that has expected your return for years.

He is the Life.
Love Him in the World of the Flesh;
And at your marriage all its occasions shall dance for joy.

CHRISTIANITY AND OTHER FAITHS

Gray's Inn Chapel: January 27th 1985

I suspect that each of us has our own experience of the difference between Britain now and Britain not so very long ago: when we were a society perfectly reflected in the 1944 Education Act, in which Religious Education was taken to be synonymous with Christian education, and when the compulsory collective daily act of worship was assumed to be a Christian act of worship. Hardly a day goes by now, for me, certainly, in which it's not made abundantly clear to me that we are inescapably a multi-racial, multi-cultural, multi-faith society.

The Vicar of St. George's, Southall, Middlesex, is now, not altogether surprisingly, Mano Rumalshah. With a name like that it's rather more surprising that he's a Christian: from South India. A few weeks ago Mano took me into the Hindu temple and Sikh gurdwara of Southall. I was given a warm welcome and generous hospitality. There are a quarter of a million Hindus and another quarter of a million Sikhs in England now. Mano, who had earlier worked in Bradford, also arranged for me to visit that much changed city, last autumn, where I had a long conversation with the President of the main mosque. There are, of course, many mosques and Urdu shops in Bradford now. There are more Muslims than Methodists in Britain today: just over a million. Leicester is the largest Hindu city outside India, with the possible exception of Durban.

If we went tomorrow to a Church of England Primary School I know in Manchester, we should find it had 9 West Indian children, 7 Hindus, 14 Sikhs, 124 Muslims, and the remaining 68 children English. The Head Teacher is a superb person. She has had to cope with a whole range of problems: the Muslim girls' dress for physical education; the need for the school canteen to respect the different dietary requirements of the different faiths; and, of course, the different religions' different feasts require different preparation, though they're celebrated by one and all. Positively, you can say it's a wonderful preparation for membership of today's world family; but not everyone looks on it quite like that. Some people bitterly resent what has happened. In Stepney, one Church of England school I know is now 98% Muslim; another is 85% Muslim; and in another part of Stepney there's a road with an almost entirely Asian state school on one side of the road and a Church of England primary school, which is almost entirely white and Afro-Caribbean, on the other. 13,000 of the 137,000 population of Tower Hamlets are now Bangladeshi.

The change in the religious situation in Britain is due, of course, not simply to what has happened here. It wasn't long ago that you got on a P & O boat to see a Buddhist. You went to the Middle East to see a Muslim. You went to India to see a Hindu. Sikhism was for the Sikhs in the Punjab. Shintoism was for the Japanese, who were not to be found anywhere near South Wales or Middlesbrough. But now there are 5 million Muslims in Europe; 2 million of them in France. Practitioners of yoga and zen abound, and not only on the wilder shores of California. At the same time, Christianity, in one of its Westernized forms, exists in the heartlands of Hinduism, Buddhism and Islam.

And it's not only Christianity which has its missionaries. A year ago I visited in Colombo a training centre for Buddhist missionaries. Many of them were bound for West Kensington and Chiswick; and I now have a very good friend amongst the monks at the Buddhist Vihara there.

Now, among Nash's terraces surrounding Regent's Park, brightly shines the great gold dome of the splendid Mosque and the Imam there is a remarkable spiritual leader. Many British people say "Aha! Arab oil!" as they drive past the Mosque. It's an interesting question how much the renewal of Islam is due to spiritual forces and how much to oil — as interesting as the question used to be: "How much is Christian influence due to spiritual forces and how much to Empire Trade?"

Which reminds one that not long ago most Hindus were under the British Raj. At that time, as some of you will know, many British children were brought up in India, and there was never any question then and there of their being brought up in the religion of the host country. But I meet a lot of people who nevertheless take it for granted that Indians in England should be prepared to be brought

103

up as Christians. In fact, quite a lot of parents of other faiths often seem to prefer their children to go to a church school — Catholic or Church of England — rather than a state school, because at least there's a belief in God expressed in the school worship and education; though sometimes Muslims, for instance, want a separate school for those of their own faith — just as there are Church of England and Roman Catholic schools. The President of the Mosque in Bradford treated me immediately as a friend and ally who would help secure justice for his people, because he assumed that we had religion in common over against the secular world.

In this new context, how should Christians behave?

For myself, I think it's very important to get rid of any of the assumed "top-dog-ness", which belongs more to the British Raj than to the Christian faith. It's also important to be particularly aware of the divisiveness of religion. Catholic and Protestant divisions in Ireland, Scotland and Liverpool remind Christians today that they are not now, and never have been free of blame in this regard; but the heart of the Sermon on the Mount is surely that followers of Christ are essentially peace-*makers*.

Sometimes, advocacy of this essentially peace-making attitude to other religions causes other Christians to accuse one of being a "syncretist" — which means, I suppose, a religious "wet": one who believes "we're all going the same way, so why worry?": one who believes in the Highest Common Factor (or is it the Lowest Common Multiple?) of religions.

I don't think that is either an accurate or a fair description of what I believe. But I do unashamedly believe in dialogue with people of other religions. I'm fascinated that the word that describes what St. Paul was doing, in the 17th Chapter of the Acts of the Apostles, translated "disputing" in the Authorised Version of the Bible, is translated "continued to hold discussions" in the New English Bible. And the Greek words *dialegomai* and *dialogizomai* can be translated either way. Clearly they imply dialogue.

For me, dialogue begins whenever I meet someone else. It's taken further when I've been with them long enough for there to be some mutual understanding and trust; and often that comes not through a great deal of talk but through working together. It's only intellectuals who believe that religion concerns primarily the assent of the intellect to a series of propositions. People of other faiths should not exist primarily in books: least of all books of doctrine. They need to be people you meet in shops, or down the street, or stand with in the unemployment queue. Above all you need to have a few meals with them. Then you begin to understand what they are, and why they are what they are, and what they believe. There's a marvellous

psychology in the insistence that young lawyers of different races,
religions and social classes should *dine* here together.

I note that St. Paul was prepared to stay in most places two years,
and spent much of that time in discussion with the Jews in the
Synagogue. When he was with Greeks he went to what is translated
the "Hall of Tyrannus", but *schole* is much better translated "school".
He went to people in their situations, and discussed with them the
meaning of the Kingdom of God.

There is one other fact that I find it helpful to consider in this
matter of "other Faiths": what we call "the accident of birth". It is
an extraordinary thing that you and I were born where we were born,
and when we were born, and with the gender we have, and the genes.
It's not easy for me to imagine myself being born in, say, China in
the 3rd Century B.C., instead of being born in Dagenham in 1925.
But that accident makes me revere the creating God and expect to
find Him revealed just as much in a Chinese person or an Arab as
in myself. I believe my God to be the God of all who dwell on the
face of the earth and of all who ever have done or ever shall. Had I
been born in France I would probably have been a Roman Catholic,
and had I been born in Palestine I would probably have been a Jew
— or, of course, an Arab.

I wouldn't be what I am, a priest in the Christian Church, if I did
not believe certain things about God who is revealed in the Old
Testament — which gives me so much in common with the 385,000
Jews living in Britain today; and if I did not believe certain things
about Jesus Christ. But I do not believe that "the Light which lightens
every man" suddenly ceased to do so when he shone in fullest
radiance in one human life.

I have an aged friend, Bishop George Appleton, who served in
Rangoon for twenty years and later was Archbishop of Perth,
Australia, and then of Jerusalem. Bishop George knows more about
"other faiths" than most people: Buddhists, Hindus, Arabs, Jews,
and so on. But he also know more about prayer than most people,
and believes that you understand a person's religion rather more by
entering with them into their prayer and worship than by studying
intellectual definitions of what they believe. His book of prayers
Praying with Others is one of the best books of prayer I know. One
particular prayer of his says almost all I want to say about
"Christianity and Other Faiths";-

O God, I gaze in wonder at thy creative love;
at thy seeking for people everywhere
and their search for thee,
showing thyself in ways they can understand.
Help me to learn more of thee from the experience of other

communities of faith,
and so to live and love that others may learn to share what
  I have found of thee in Jesus Christ.
Open my eyes; enlighten my mind; enlarge my heart;
  and grant that my own expression of thee in life and word
  may come closer to thy eternal truth and love:
  O God, *my* God, God of *all*.

Amen.

MARTIN BUBER

Gray's Inn Chapel: February 3rd 1985

I want to preach to you today about a Jewish thinker and theologian whom I have great reason to revere and, indeed, to whom I owe much.

In 1940 Bishop John Robinson, author of *Honest to God*, then a young student at Cambridge, was handed a copy of Martin Buber's dull-brown paper-back *I and Thou*, which John later admitted "transformed him".

Nearly twenty years later, I remember the United Nations Secretary-General Dag Hammarskjöld coming to Cambridge to receive an Honorary Degree and paying tribute there to what Martin Buber meant to him — indeed, in the last days of his life, until his plane crashed in the Congo, Hammarskjöld had been working on a translation into Swedish of *I and Thou*. I have spoken in Chapel on another occasion about what Hammarskjöld owed to Buber. Who was this man, Martin Buber? And why is it that many still believe his book *I and Thou*, if it were really understood, could have far reaching consequences for our time?

Buber was born in Vienna in 1878: a Jew through and through; the product of the finest liberal intellectual background. As a student, he was caught up in the beginnings of the Zionist movement, but its fervid nationalism alienated him from its aims and from further active association. He felt the need for the revitalisation of the spiritual and cultural arteries of Zionism. Likewise, his disappointment at a young age with Orthodox Judaism was signalled by his lapsing from formal practice, which continued to the end of his life. Buber found much of formal religion hard to take, and indeed sometimes irrelevant to what he perceived as the central aim of human existence: to establish a relationship with what he called the "Eternal Thou". Buber was a man who was intensely alive and aware; and this awareness made him impatient with words, forms and processes which had become unhinged from what he regarded as the core of being. So, though a Jew, brought up in all the traditions of Judaism, he rejected much of this in order to seek a core of vitality which he could accept not only on the intellectual plane but at every other level of his being. This was the beginning of what he was later to call "the Total Response".

Refusing the comfort of dogma and the support of popular nationalism he determined to follow the truth wherever it might lead. It led, in fact, to an encounter with Hasidism: a mystical movement which had developed particularly amongst the Jews of southern Poland in the 18th Century. Buber became a sophisticated exponent of Hasidism. From 1923 to 1933 he taught at the University of Frankfurt; from 1938 to 1951 he was Professor of Social Philosophy at the Hebrew University, Jerusalem. He died in 1965.

Buber came to believe there is a divine spark in every human being. These sparks are isolated by shells which enclose each person as with armour. But there is a way of life by which a man can cast off these shells and break their confining embrace. Buber believed we should obey the precept "Love your neighbour as yourself" not simply because it is a commandment of God, but because through it and in it we *meet* God. "Existence" he wrote "will remain meaningless for you if you yourself do not penetrate it with active love and if you do not in this way discover meaning for yourself. Everything is waiting to be hallowed by you. Meet the world with the fulness of your being and you shall meet God. If you wish to believe, Love".

It was in 1916 that Buber made a preliminary sketch of *I and Thou*, a first draft of what was eventually a volume of little more than a hundred pages when it was printed in 1922. It was translated into English fifteen years later. In a sense, *I and Thou* is as much poetry as philosophy. Certainly it does not disclose its full meaning on first reading.

The world, Buber tells us, has a two-fold meaning. To understand this two-fold nature of human existence is the beginning of wisdom. It's two-fold aspect is expressed in the fundamental difference between our relation to persons and to things. That is not precisely Buber's language. He speaks of the difference between our relation to the world of "Thou" and our relation to the world of "it".

Of course, what he has to say is more complex than that, not least because persons may be, and for certain purposes must be, treated as things: when, for instance, a surgeon operates upon someone who is unconscious; and animate and inanimate nature can sometimes confront us with an almost personal approach and demand from us something like a personal response.

But by and large to the world of things, of "It", belongs the whole domain over which science reigns and the world of technology. The world which we use belongs to that world. *Par excellence*, these days, we can say it's the computer world.

Yet man's life does not consist primarily of that "It' world. In relation to that world man may be master. He can collect, control, observe, measure, weigh, arrange and order it. But in the encounter with a person he is no longer in sole control. He is addressed and has to respond. He meets the other, once he does not treat that person as a thing. He passes from his solitariness into community, where there is not one point of view but two or more.

Buber said: "All real life is meeting". And it is through our response to other persons that we become persons. It is others who challenge, enlighten and enrich us. We are persons, in the end, only because of and through our relations with other persons. Through sharing in the giving and receiving between persons, the "I" becomes real.

We prefer sometimes to wrap ourselves in our solitariness and pursue our solitary purposes: afraid to launch into meeting. There are others, and they can be very dangerous, even very evil, who simply treat other persons as things: untrusting, uncaring bosses; and we can all build round ourselves a wall of ideas: a philosophy, a theology, a tradition, a ritual, a point of view. When you work in a university you soon realise that quite a lot of people are avoiding life by pursuing "subjects". But in every profession there are ways of avoiding the "I-Thou" relationship. I imagine the Law has at least some aspects that can tempt one that way. Nothing can reach us if we build up a kind of impersonal mesh. We can take refuge in a world where we are safe from the disturbing challenge of "Thou".

But if I am to grow I must become aware of a "Thou" who never ceases to summon me forth into existence.

It is easy to see how the world of the computer and bureaucratic administration, the realm of the "I-it", can be so attractive. I may use it, exploit it, experience it pleasurably. In a word, it is power: seductive power.

It is easy to see how a young medical student, at first feeling a vocation to help and cure suffering humanity, once he has become a doctor in a crowded and busy hospital, under pressure, can cease to devote the necessary and appropriate time to every patient. Suffering human beings become simply objects. They recede to the world of "It". This is the tragedy of being human. The marriage which began with "I-Thou", declines into scarcely more than "I-it". Buber says that in order to avoid losing the "I-Thou", we must make our stand on the narrow ridge as a company of soldiers takes up its position on an embattled hill and says "From here we will not retreat". That narrow ridge is the meeting place of the "We". Only those who are capable of saying "Thou" to one another can truly say "We".

I began by saying that Buber's book *I and Thou*, if it were really understood, could have far reaching consequences for our time.

There are at least three reasons for my saying, and believing, that.

The first I have already suggested. This is clearly the age of the computer: in very many ways a blessing. But few things in this world are simply blessing. There is in this world a curse side to almost every blessing. The computer could be the curse of our age, unless with and alongside the growth of the power of this so to speak "I-it" machine there is a corresponding growth in our development of the "I-Thou" aspect of our lives.

My second reason is like unto it, namely this. At the moment I see, week by week, a good deal of the unemployed in our big cities. That unemployment is in part due to the advent of the computer. The underlying assumption of the "I-it" world is that people are less important than the jobs they do; whereas the person who has discovered the "I-Thou" relationship knows that men and women are essentially and inalienably persons, meant to live in personal fellowship with one another; and that the services which they have to perform in society, however important they may be, are to some extent incidental and subordinate to this personal life. It is a huge message, which needs to be conveyed at the moment to each one of the over four million people of our nation who are unemployed: that they may be unemployed, but the capacity they have been given for "I-Thou" relationship crowns each one of them with a glory which cannot be taken away. This must never be used as a reason for keeping people unemployed; but it may enable them whilst unemployed to shine like the stars they are.

There is a third reason. In the end, all true religion is a matter of the "I-Thou" relationship. Divine Service is a mockery and a sham if it is not the expression of a fundamental "I-Thou" relationship with the Eternal "Thou". How easy it is to make of a service an "I-it" relationship! We simply say a set pattern of words, listen to this and that, and "go through the motions".

But Buber would have us go further even than that. He would say — and I set myself humbly alongside him — that true religion is never primarily about "services". It is about living day in day out in the dimension of the "Thou". That dimension enables us to set our "I-It" relationships in their proper perspective. But first and foremost we need to recognise a call coming from the Eternal "Thou" — to whom we must respond, and, in responding, discover growingly who we are, until we are called out of this world into a new relationship with the Eternal "Thou". And all our human relationships and our very capacity to relate, are in some way not only of I to thou, but of the Eternal "Thou" in me to the Eternal "Thou" in thee.

Buber was a Jew. But certainly he speaks powerfully to me. It is just as though he were St. John, writing: "He that loveth not abideth in death".

The Eternal "Thou" is the Source, the Continuing and the Beyond of the life of each one of us.

A PASSAGE TO INDIA

Gray's Inn Chapel: April 28th 1985

I very much wanted to see the film of *A Passage to India*, not least because, after several visits, India will always have a bit of my heart; but also because, when I was Chaplain of Trinity, I used to relieve the Chaplain of King's on Thursday afternoons and sing Evensong for him in that glorious Chapel; and E.M. Forster, although an avowed agnostic, would often attend — for purely aesthetic reasons, he would aver. He was by then not far off eighty, and, as Simon Raven wrote of him in those years: "Morgan Forster was (or seemed to be) bone idle . . . for ever pottering from nowhere in particular to nowhere else". (But isn't that what those near eighty should be encouraged to do?!)

But is there a sermon, you may ask, in the film of a novel by an avowed agnostic?

I have never myself taken the view that an agnostic or an atheist has nothing to teach us about God; nor do I believe that artists, composers and novelists, if they do not believe in God, will have nothing of God to reveal to us in their work. And, in fact, I found that God had a good deal to say to me through David Lean's very remarkable film.

It was in 1906 that Forster became tutor and friend of Syed Ross Masood, a rich young Muslim from Aligarh, not far south of Delhi, who was waiting at Weybridge to go up to Oxford. That friendship altered Forster's life. So, when he first visited India, six years later, he had already had a closer relationship with an Indian than many of the ruling British in India were ever likely to achieve; if indeed they thought such a relationship desirable. It meant that Forster was outraged by the accepted boundaries of contact between the British and the Indian. Forster's friend Masood had a whole repertoire of stories of slights he had received in his home country from the British.

112

But when I think of what God seemed to be saying to me through *A Passage to India*, I would want to pause there; for in these days, when there is a whole race relations industry, and rightly so, Forster is I think right to suggest that friendship is the best door to race relations. I count it a huge privilege to have friendships with Ugandans, Nigerians, Indians, Sri Lankans and West Indians: mostly former parishioners or former undergraduates. And it is those friendships which make me as outraged as Forster when I find people treated as "lesser breeds" because of their race and colour. If only people could and would make personal friends across the barriers of race and colour, those barriers and boundaries would rapidly be seen to be the utter irrelevance they are.

Nevertheless, it could be said that drawn to India by friendship, it was, in a sense easier for Forster. Others were there to bring order where there was often chaos, or at least muddle and squalor.

When first Forster visited India, in 1912, independence was a distant ideal. When he visited it a second time, in 1921, (as a Maharajah's secretary, though still with little concern for politics) it was a time of high political drama. Gandhi had emerged as a leader. The British Government had published the Montagu-Chelmsford proposals for the sharing of Government between British and Indians. When *A Passage to India* was published, in 1924, the rights and wrongs of the British raj were much in the news.

There is no denying that there was a good deal that was wrong in British colonial government, not least in India; but you get glimpses in *A Passage to India* of the good there was in the *Pax Britannica*. Medicine, which had trained people like Dr Aziz, owed much to Britain. Education, which eventually brought Masood to Oxford, owed as much; and the courts, even the court proceedings at the mythical court of Chandrapore, owed much to Britain; and the civil service; and, of course, the railways: not least the train which took Aziz and his party up to the Marabar Hills.

God in friendship. Yes. But God also in order out of chaos, and in good government. That, too, is important. Aziz recognises that "India's a muddle". But then, and now, that muddle in India meant suffering and death: deaths like those in the riots in Ahmedabad only this last week. God and government: a very important theme; and the more so now that India's population is over 700 million compared with a mere 200 million when Forster first visited India. God and government: a very important theme, here as much as in India.

For Forster, the foreign was fascinating. He had a sympathy for the outsider. Friendship gave him a perception of people and places, an understanding of attitudes and ideas, which many of his contemporaries would have rejected as worthless or irrelevant.

He portrays Mrs Moore, bored to tears with the amateur dramatics at the Club at Chandrapore, slipping out and wandering into a mosque close by, interrupting Aziz at his meditations. Aziz at first tells her abruptly that she has no right there, and says: "This is a holy place for Moslems". Mrs Moore gently replies: "God is here". And with that remark their friendship begins. "I shall tell my community — our friends — about you" Aziz exclaims excitedly. "That God is here — very good, very fine indeed" he says.

Perhaps, sixty years on, here and now, in England, we need to reflect on what Mrs Moore had to say.

"I like mysteries" says Mrs Moore "but I rather dislike muddles". "A mystery is only a high sounding term for a muddle" replies Mr Fielding. But he is wrong. Mystery lies at the heart of all true religions: all the great religions. And that kind of mystery is not simply "muddle".

There are many other incidents and passages in Forster's cleverly titled *A Passage to India* which are profoundly religious even though he skilfully cloaks them in the simplest narrative.

Ronny, Mrs Moore's son, is the City Magistrate of Chandrapore.

"We're not out here" he says "for the purpose of behaving pleasantly! . . . We're out here to do justice and keep the peace".

"The English *are* out here to be pleasant", his mother insists. "How do you make that out, mother?" asks Ronny gently. "Because India is part of the earth. And God has put us on the earth in order to be pleasant to each other. God . . . is . . . love." She hesitated, seeing how much he disliked the argument, but something made her go on. "God has put us on earth to love our neighbours and to show it, and He is omnipresent, even in India, to see how we are succeeding . . ."

He waited until she had done, and then said gently, "I quite see that. I suppose I ought to get off to my files now, and you'll be going to bed."

"I suppose so, I suppose so" said his mother.

They did not part for a few minutes, but the conversation had become unreal since Christianity had entered it. Ronny approved of religion as long as it endorsed the National Anthem, but he objected to it when it attempted to influence his life. Then he would say in respectful yet decided tones, "I don't think it does to talk about these things, every fellow has to work out his own religion", and any fellow who heard him muttered "Hear!"

Mrs Moore felt that she had made a mistake in mentioning God, but she found him increasingly difficult to avoid as she grew older, and he had been constantly in her thoughts since she entered India . . .

What an odd passage for an avowed agnostic to write!

But it is not so odd or contradictory to me, if I see in my mind's eye that timid old man making his way slowly through the candlelight at King's, as Evensong is about to begin, to sit in the carved choir stalls he so loved.

Most of us who are good at words know well that however good we are at describing muddles, words fail when it comes to those mysteries that inspire and animate the great authors, the great civilisations, the great religions — and people like you and me.

A Passage to India is, at least in part, a modern parable.

In the final Court scene, Forster concentrates our attention first of all on one man who has no bearing officially upon the trial: the man who pulled the "punkah" over the court that kept the bigwigs cool:

> "The Court was crowded and of course very hot, and the first person Adela noticed in it was the humblest of all who were present, a person who had no bearing officially upon the trial: the man who pulled the punkah. Almost naked, and splendidly formed, he sat on a raised platform near the back, in the middle of the central gangway . . . He had the strength and beauty that sometimes come to flower in Indians of low birth. When that strange race nears the dust and is condemned as untouchable, then nature remembers the physical perfection that she accomplished elsewhere, and throws out a god — not many, but one here and there, to prove to society how little its categories impress her. This man would have been notable anywhere; among the thin-hammed, flat-chested mediocrities of Chandrapore he stood out as divine, yet he was of the city, its garbage had nourished him, he would end on its rubbish heaps. Pulling the rope towards him, relaxing it rhythmically, sending swirls of air over others, receiving none himself, he seemed apart from human destinies, a male fate, a winnower of souls. Opposite him, also on a platform, sat the little assistant magistrate, cultivated, self-conscious and conscientious. The punkah wallah was none of these things; he scarcely knew that he existed and did not understand why the Court was fuller than usual, indeed he did not know that it was fuller than usual, didn't even know he worked a fan, though he thought he pulled a rope".

Forster draws attention to him in order to question the importance, the self-importance, of the other people in the Court.

The very existence of the punkah wallah puts down the mighty from their seat and exalts the humble and meek.

Indeed, a few paragraphs after Forster's description of the punkah wallah, he has those in the body of the Court request that the English woman, who is accusing Dr Aziz of a criminal offence, be given a seat on the platform; and when he grants permission, other European ladies and gentlemen join her on the platform, until the Magistrate insists they literally climb down. "A platform", he says, "confers authority".

Here again is something for us to meditate on today.

It is very easy in Britain today to have a kind of map of powerful and important people: Her Majesty the Queen, the Prime Minister, Judges, the Bishops, City Directors: and then, at the bottom of the pile — the unemployed. But that is not how Jesus saw people. And in *A Passage to India* the agnostic Forster caught something of the heart of the Gospel of Jesus Christ our Lord.

AN APPROPRIATE PATRIOTISM

Gray's Inn Chapel: November 10th 1985

"Who is here so vile that will not love his country?" That question is surely appropriately asked, and answered, on Remembrance Sunday.

But let me remind you that Shakespeare put that marvellous question into the mouth of Brutus: "the noblest Roman of them all", but the assassin of his country's Caesar. So Shakespeare warns us that it is not always easy to discover an "appropriate patriotism".

Yet the question of an "appropriate patriotism" is, I believe, an urgent and important question for every one of us in Britain today; and not least for those of us who confess and call ourselves Christians.

I have recently returned from Middlesbrough, which has the highest unemployment in our country, much of it long term; and the outlook is bleak. There are housing estates there of 70% unemployment. Yet I found there amongst the people a fierce love of their locality, Teesside, coupled sometimes with a bitterness because people in the South seem often to them no longer to care about people in the North. It is a commonplace now that Britain is divided not only between rich and poor but between North and South. Not only 'regionalism', but the disparities between the regions, introduce, at the least, uncertainties into the idea of national loyalty today.

And now that we are part of Europe, and governed not least by the Treaty of Rome — and, of course, by the gnomes of Zurich! — that, too, complicates the question of an "appropriate patriotism".

And the recent lobby on World Development at the House of Commons made clear how many people nowadays, and many of them Christians, have a strong trans-national loyalty, which transcends, even if it includes, national loyalty.

117

Again: I have met a number of people in the last years who were, in some paradoxical way, devoutly thankful for the Falklands crisis, whatever its cost, not least because it seemed to clarify for them the question of love of country in a way in which it seemed not to have been clear for nearly forty years, since the end of the Second World War. There is little doubt of most people's patriotism in time of war. *Dulce et decorum est pro patria mori* was an honoured saying for twenty centuries and more: until the Great War poet Wilfred Owen called it "the old lie".

I think I should share with you the perplexity I had at the time of the Falklands crisis. For as Director of *Christian Action* I had to give a good deal of attention to the subject of Diego Garcia, which many of you will know is an island in the Indian Ocean of virtually the same size and population as the Falklands. The islanders of Diego Garcia, British subjects all of them, had lived an exemplary peaceful life, but their continued presence on their island was deemed by Britain in 1966 incompatible with our military interests, and, by a combination of cajolery, deception, economic pressure and sheer force, the whole population was compelled to transfer to the island of Mauritius, 500 miles away, where they are now effectively refugees. Few in Britain at the time noticed or took up their cause. The people of the island were black. And it was in the spring of 1982, virtually the eve of the Falklands crisis, that the question of financial compensation for the islanders was eventually dealt with, in lieu of the possibility of any other form of compensation. The phrase "the wishes of the islanders themselves must be paramount" is therefore one that is bound to raise a smile, albeit a cynical smile, on the lips of the erstwhile inhabitants of Diego Garcia and of any who know of and are concerned with their plight, and to complicate the question of an "appropriate patriotism".

To give just one more illustration: I shall never forget as a young Chaplain of Trinity sitting next to Otto Frisch, the Jacksonian Professor of Physics, a Fellow of the College, at dinner one evening. Frisch — of whom I have spoken in Chapel before — had been involved in making the first atomic bomb at Los Alamos in the deserts of New Mexico. That evening he told me his shock and dismay when he heard General Groves, the United States General in overall charge of the atomic bomb project, say to the British scientist Sir James Chadwick (who had discovered the neutron): "You realise of course that the whole purpose of our working on this project is to subdue the Russians" — a remark which was made when the Russians were supposed to be our allies. Frisch said he suddenly realised that the purpose of the project was different from how he had been led to perceive it. As a refugee from Hitler's Germany he had of course been glad to be involved in playing his part in defeating Nazism.

An "appropriate patriotism" was certainly complex for Otto Frisch, more than once.

The comedian Norman Wisdom, living now in semi-retirement on the Isle of Man, said in a recent broadcast: "I like this island. I like the country: away from strikes, burglaries, muggings, vandalism, greed and lack of discipline. I love Britain; but I love it the way it should be, the way it used to be, the way the Isle of Man still is".

But at least the wisdom of Norman Wisdom — to love Britain "the way it should be" — means that patriotism for him involves having a vision of and for his country. For the Christian, patriotism and vision certainly go together. Our patriotism has constantly to be shot through with that vision given us in the Old Testament, when "swords shall be beaten into ploughshares and spears into pruning hooks" — and in the New Testament: the vision of the New Jerusalem.

An "appropriate patriotism" is, of course, more difficult at a time of national decline. Immediately after the Second World War, Britain ruled about 550 million people: a quarter of the population of the globe. Now it rules about 55 million: a tenth of what it did; and the world's population has doubled.

Different people have, of course, different ways of expressing what their country means to them. England means to many the White Cliffs of Dover; Shakespeare; "I vow to thee my country" sung to Gustav Holst's tune at a Royal Wedding; an English garden and an English rose; the Choir of King's Cambridge at Christmas — and the Cenotaph in Whitehall.

But having met with a lot of young people in the last years in the most deprived areas of the country — in Liverpool, Manchester, Leeds, Bradford, Coventry, Birmingham, to say nothing of London — I have to say that what is abundantly clear is that that kind of patriotism means little or nothing to very many of them. They are alienated from all that, and that kind of patriotism is alien to them. "Alienated" is the word I would use to describe hosts of young people in our most deprived cities: thousands of them. Britain, they feel, belongs to other people: to a power group to which they have no access.

And that word "alien" itself adds one more ingredient to this difficult question of an "appropriate patriotism".

The National Front is clear what "being British" is all about; and their vision does not include a lot of people who by race or colour do not seem to them immediately British. But for every member of the National Front in Britain today there are a hundred people, maybe a thousand, who have no time for the National Front, but

119

entertain nevertheless, where race and colour are concerned, not altogether dissimilar ideas, if not in theory then in practice. For the Christian, the vision is clear. "In Christ there is no East nor West". "He has made of one blood all the nations of men to dwell on the face of the earth".

By an "appropriate patriotism" we must surely mean something that will enable a black or white 18-year-old unemployed boy in, say, Brixton, born in this country, to see this country today as for him a "land of hope and glory".

I have already said that the idea of an "appropriate patriotism" is complex; and it is not easy to get across or put into practice. But to accept the idea of a large alienated body of young people as permanently part of our country would to my mind be evidently evil.

So I have had to say to myself, as I say to you, given the difficulties of an "appropriate patriotism", how do I, as a Christian, guide people towards one?

The question with which I began is not irrelevant: for it suggests that it is not always the most obvious patriot who is the true patriot.

One of my greatest heroes is Dietrich Bonhoeffer, the Lutheran theologian, hanged by the Nazis for his part in the conspiracy against Hitler. Bonhoeffer gave his life for love of his country. He was the true patriot: the true German imprisoned and hanged by his own countrymen.

In 1937 there was held in this country the Oxford Conference on "Church, Community and State". Bonhoeffer was one of the German delegates prevented from attending it. There is a paragraph in the Conference Report which was intended to assist those in Germany who were fighting Hitler. It helps us today, I believe, to discern as Christians what may be a true patriotism in our own country. It states:

> The love of the Christian for his people should therefore be part of his gratitude to God for the riches which are his through the community in which he has been born. As with every divine gift, the gift of national community has been and is being abused by men, and made to serve sin. Any form of national egotism, whereby the love of one's own people leads to the suppression of other nationalities or national minorities, or the failure to respect and appreciate the gifts of other people, is sin and rebellion against God, who is the Creator and Lord of all peoples.

A healthy nation can only be one that helps all its people to play their full part in the life of the nation.

Britain, I want to say, cannot be loved too much, providing that love is the kind of love Dietrich Bonhoeffer had for his country: the love that asks many questions about the nation's polarisation, about those who are in poverty and powerless, about the inequality and injustice in our land.

Christians are not strangers to the idea of a patriot who has to speak unpalatable truth to his nation; for our very faith is founded, as Dietrich Bonhoeffer well knew, upon Him who witnessed to the truth, held out the truth to his own nation, and for that truth suffered triumphantly death upon a Cross, and "as a Victim won the day".

I have said earlier that our patriotism must be shot through with our vision of the New Jerusalem. Perhaps, then, on this Remembrance Day, not least in gratitude for those who died that we might live, we should sum up our thoughts and prayers and aspirations by singing with new resolve and dedication those words of that great Englishman William Blake which we now call simply "Jerusalem".

And did those feet in ancient time
    Walk upon England's mountains green?
And was the holy Lamb of God
    On England's pleasant pastures seen?
And did the countenance divine
    Shine forth upon our clouded hills?
And was Jerusalem builded here
    Among those dark satanic mills?

Bring me my bow of burning gold!
    Bring me my arrows of desire!
Bring me my spear! O clouds, unfold!
    Bring me my chariot of fire!
I will not cease from mental fight,
    Nor shall my sword sleep in my hand,
Till we have built Jerusalem
    In England's green and pleasant land.

THE GOOD SAMARITAN TODAY

Gray's Inn Chapel: January 26th 1986

I wonder whether you find, as I do, that however many times you hear the story of the Good Samaritan, it has something fresh to say to you?

Of course, the fact that it is someone versed in the Law who asks Jesus the question "Who is my neighbour?" makes the question, and the answer, particularly relevant here. (And who but a Lawyer would have asked: "What shall I do to *inherit* eternal life?") But it's more than merely a Lawyer's question: more than a professional's quest for a precise answer: a question of "limited liability". It's the kind of cover up, the attempt to evade responsibility, which I've met with again and again in what Bishop David Sheppard calls "Comfortable Britain": "Are the unemployed in Liverpool really my responsibility?" Martin Luther King says the Lawyer's question epitomises the "paralysis of analysis".

But Jesus catches the question in mid-air, so to speak, and brings it right down to earth, everyone's earth, in an event which could easily happen in many parts of the world today. He describes a mugging, where a mugging was part of the scene.

We don't know, and we don't need to know, who was mugged, or where. In a sense, the man who was mugged is any victim: anyone who's *down* and *out*; anyone in need; anyone who confronts us on our road in their need: he — or she — is our neighbour.

The Priest and the Levite "pass by on the other side". I've heard the suggestion that they were hurrying to a committee meeting in Jericho to discuss the problems of mugging on the Jerusalem-Jericho road. (A High Priest's Commission on Urban Priority Areas?)

The suggestion is more entertaining than convincing. But it does make me want to press the question: Why did they — the Priest and the Levite (and *not* the Samaritan) — why do we — pass by on the other side of those in need? That question is very important for our whole Church and Nation just now.

It was surely not because the Priest and the Levite were evil that they passed by. Presumably Jesus chose them to represent respectable and respected people: well brought up, well educated, and religious — like the Lawyer. It was, and is, I believe, more likely some self-regarding fear in them — and us. They didn't want to see, couldn't allow themselves to see, the man who'd been mugged, for fear of what seeing might entail. Of course, in one sense they saw him. (The parable says so.) People often these days see — on TV, in the newspapers, or even in the streets — and fear: fear to get involved when they see someone in need. And there are realities to people's fears. The man "fell among *robbers*" — plural.

Not far from where I live in South London there's a lot of "gentrification" going on. There was a proposal to set up a hostel for homeless young people. Many of the gentrified were petrified — and opposed the scheme. They were frightened of having "another world" just across the road.

But the Samaritan, the stranger-within-the-gates — in spite of the robbers, and the man who's been mugged lying half dead — he saw and crossed over. What he saw made him come alongside the man in need.

The Jews had been taught to care particularly for the stranger-within-their-gates. And Jesus would have got a smile out of his audience when he told them it was the stranger-within-the-gates — the immigrant, so to speak — who in this instance did the caring. It would have jolted a good many who presumed they were the caring, not the cared for. And there's something here for all of us who are "caring professionals" in one form or another, maybe simply by our Christian profession.

I find myself wondering why the stranger-within-the-gates crossed over, but neither the Priest nor the Levite. *"Why did the Samaritan cross the road?"* is almost the central unspoken question of this parable. Was it that, even in those days, the Samaritan knew something of what it was to be wounded because he was on the fringe — even beyond the fringe — of society? — an outsider — as many of our immigrants feel themselves to be. (The Jews, we are told, had "no dealings with the Samaritans"). Perhaps vulnerability — indeed, being wounded — had taught the Samaritan compassion. It often does, when it doesn't embitter.

The stranger on that road shows a care beyond religion — and more than religion. He's the very picture of that self-giving which every human being has within them. He shows a daring, dangerous, courageous, self-giving: an expensive, expansive, almost excessive self-giving.

In the last years, visiting in our inner cities multi-racial communities, I've heard quite often of self-giving by people of different races and religions from my own, witnessing to our common humanity, our true humanity, and to the divine origins of our common humanity. Sometimes that self-giving has been in heroic acts, during, say, a riot; but more often in humble acts — like regular blood-doning; or like being, as an Asian, a good and caring primary school teacher or nurse or doctor, or simply befriending as a neighbour someone just out of hospital.

I met someone a few weeks ago — a Christian — on whom the truth had just dawned that the Samaritan *wasn't* a Christian. She was astonished! "But I thought the point of the story was that the Samaritan was a Christian" she said. "No. The point of the story is that the Samaritan was a Samaritan" I replied.

But Jesus isn't simply telling us a rattling good story about someone who's a particularly good example of self-giving and care in a bygone age. He's talking, in a parable, about the divine self-giving, the divine compassion, which lies at the heart of us all, of everyone coming into the world.

If you like, he's talking — unselfconsciously — about himself: about the Crossing of the Road which beggars description, but which St. Paul had a shot at describing when he wrote of him who:

> being in the form of God,
> thought it not robbery to be equal with God:
> but made himself of no reputation,
> and took upon him the form of a servant,
> and was made in the likeness of man:
> and being found in fashion as a man,
> he humbled himself,
> and became obedient unto death,
> even the death of the cross.

There never was, and there never will be, a Crossing of the Road like that. He came where we are and had compassion on us — literally. He suffered alongside us — that's the meaning of the word "compassion": he suffered alongside us even the death of the cross; so that the Christ-figure in the parable is not only the Samaritan but the victim: the man mugged on the Jerusalem road.

There's a cathedral in France with a series of stained glass windows that wonderfully depict the story of the Samaritan. But the halo in one of them is not over the Samaritan but over the victim: reminding all who gaze at the glass of Him who "as a Victim won the day". Going round the urban priority areas in these last years, I can't tell you how much I've received from the *victims* of our society: the powerless, the wounded. None of us, I believe, can give much, do much, till we've learnt to receive — not least from the wounded and the victims.

Three more thoughts this parable provokes in me:

First: The parable is about what is sometimes called a one-to-one relationship: a man who's been mugged and a Samaritan who ministers to him. But supposing the victim was in, say, the Sudan and the Samaritan in London? Out of sight: out of mind? Supposing, to use the phrase of St. Paul, the "Form of the Servant" has to take the form of the civil servant, and the help of the Samaritan has to be given not by an individual but by a group of people, maybe by an organisation? (*The Samaritans* are not only individuals but an organisation.) Supposing the help of the Samaritan needs a Bill got through Parliament?

Shaftesbury was a Samaritan to the children of the slums of Britain a century ago by his political actions. If we see politics in the light of the Samaritan it can no longer be simply "a dirty game". If we see policing in the light of the Samaritan, the Police *Force* has always essentially to be a force for care, protection, compassion: for order out of chaos. If we see the whole organisation of the Health *Service* in the light of the Samaritan, we shall see its inequities and inadequacies — and its merits and glories — in a new light.

The Christian has to work out what it means to be a Samaritan both in the private and personal world and in the public and ultimately no less personal world.

This becomes abundantly clear when you are face to face with, say, someone in long-term unemployment. The man in Liverpool who said "I'm forty so I'm finished" — he'd been told he was "unskilled", not likely to get another job, and need not register more than once every three months — such a man needs, of course, one-to-one attention: not least someone to listen to him. But unless he is also the object of Government policy you are unlikely to be able to give him or his wife and kids long-term help.

The penultimate thought this parable provokes in me is that I would only have had half the thoughts I have had about it had I not been brought close to this unemployed person and that in these last years. "What you believe depends on where you stand". We have different thoughts, different theologies, if we stand on, say, the

125

Howrah Bridge over the Hoogli river in Calcutta from those we have if we stand in the foyer of the Hilton Hotel, Park Lane. We have different thoughts if we stand in the HQ of the DHSS to those we have if we linger in a local office amongst the queue. "Why did nobody tell me it was like this?" a Cabinet Minister was reported to have asked when he first *visited* Liverpool. When you *cross the road* you have new thoughts which lead to new actions.

My last thought is of a different order.

This parable does not only speak of God and of Christ. Because it speaks of Christ it speaks of my humanity and yours. It speaks, as I've said, of the potential of every human being. It speaks of that divine self-giving which lies at the heart of our human nature: yours and mine.

The man who is wounded and lies half dead on the road is not a figure of fiction. He's me, now, and you. He's our wounded humanity. That's why we're so sick and separated from one another in society.

This parable is not simply about our doing good to one another. It's about the wounded you and me.

But we are met here because we discern — if only dimly — that the Good Samaritan has power to bind up our wounds and pour in oil and wine. We are come into this place because He has said He will put us on His own beast, and, at the last — but not only at the last, but in the here and now — bring us to an Inn — of which the Church is the very sign and symbol — and take care of us.

The Good Samaritan is therefore, finally, a parable of Hope. It speaks to us of the divine power to heal not only individuals who are wounded and sick but a whole society and His whole world.

A.E. HOUSMAN: 1859-1936

Gray's Inn Chapel: April 27th 1986

In three days it will be half a century since the death of Alfred Edward Housman.

The largest and wealthiest of the Colleges of Cambridge, Trinity, which most of you will know extends round a lawned and cobble-stoned court — which might by itself have served as the nucleus of a Tudor village — overflowed during the 19th century even this manorial domain into a sort of Victorian tenement, wedged between two narrow arteries of traffic; and here, whether by choice or assignment, but in any case without objection, A.E. Housman established himself, in the dark honeycomb of what is called Whewell's Court. Up two flights of Staircase K, his rooms overlooked on one side the busy intersection of Sydney Street and Jesus Lane, and on the other, a shadowy enclosure adorned by the seated bronze figure of a Grecian youth, whose naked form was only at certain hours of the day touched by sunlight. Few locations in Cambridge, and none in Trinity, could have taken less advantage of the amenities that everywhere abounded; and Housman did nothing to improve the appearance of a dismally univiting apartment. Though convenient to his lecture room and dining hall, it was an abode that possessed no attraction other than bookshelves and solitude; for Housman had been quick to discourage, by his wintry and withering unsociability, all but the most persistent overtures, and to throw up that prickly barrier of reserve across which not many dared stretch a hand. Seldom visiting, he was seldom visited.

I can tell you all this, not least because, twenty years after Housman's death, I occupied rooms in Whewell's Court — on G Staircase; and, indeed, the maquette of the seated bronze figure of the Grecian youth — by the kindness of another Fellow of Trinity, George Kitson Clark, whose father had presented it to Whewell's Court — graces my Kennington sitting-room at this moment.

In 1956, Housman was still a legend, and the aged irascible Andrew Gow, also a Fellow of Trinity, crippled with arthritis, was still there to "tire the sun with talking", not least of Housman.

Such friends as Housman had at Cambridge were chosen, like the bottles in his cellar, for their subtle bouquet and rare vintage, but with the exception of Andrew Gow, none of them — I think it is true to say — had the enduring qualities of Housman's favourite burgundy. Gow, the young tutor who shared Housman's Classical knowledge but surpassed his range of aesthetic sensibility, offered him something more than fluent table-talk; and between them a spontaneous respect grew into a staunch attachment.

I have in my possession a copy of the Memorial Service to the ninety-one year old Andrew Sydenham Farrar Gow which was held in Trinity Chapel eight years ago. On a cold day in February, the wind sweeping across the Fens, that service was the most chilling I have ever known, and it ended with the singing of the bleak hymn Housman had written for, and which was first sung at, his own memorial service.

> O Thou that from thy mansion
>   Though time and place to roam,
> Dost send abroad thy children,
>   And then dost call them home,
>
> That men and tribes and nations
>   And all thy hand hath made
> May shelter them from sunshine
>   In thine eternal shade:
>
> We now to peace and darkness
>   And earth and thee restore
> Thy creature that thou madest
>   And wilt cast forth no more.

Perhaps I should remind you that much had happened to Housman before he came to Trinity.

It was in 1911 that the fifty-two year old Housman had been elected to be Kennedy Professor of Latin at Cambridge. His election was by no means inevitable: "He was undoubtedly the best man for the job" Gow said "but he had been too rude to the men he didn't like." And when the palm of victory in the election fell to Housman, his fellow candidates, even as they congratulated him, began to gird themselves for the Jovian thunderbolts to come.

Housman had come from University College, London; and the photograph of him on his departure for Cambridge is unable to conceal the weary sadness which accompanied him even in the proud flush of success.

True, his farewell after-dinner speech to University College was one of the brightest he had given. Glass in hand, he remarked: "Cambridge has seen Wordsworth drunk and Porson sober. Now I am a greater scholar than Wordsworth, and a greater poet than Porson, so I fall betwixt and between."

You may well be aware that Housman failed his finals at Oxford and spent more than ten years working near here as a clerk in the Patent Office, in which time he also worked on Ovid and Juvenal and other Classical authors; and his published articles created such an impression that in 1892 he was appointed Professor of Latin in London University.

You may also know — but it's rarely proclaimed from pulpits — that at Oxford Housman had formed a deep attachment to his contemporary, Moses Jackson, and this experience of unrequited love Housman clearly had in mind when he wrote a verse published posthumously:

Because I liked you better
    Than suits a man to say,
It irked you, and I promised
    To throw the thought away.

Well, you may ask, why do you pick up that thought and put it into a sermon? — if indeed what I have said so far can begin to be called a sermon.

I have said what I have said so far because it is important, I believe, that we should let the light of the Gospel fall on the memory of Housman, for there is much we can learn thereby.

We most of us go on remembering Housman not primarily because of the several volumes of his edition of Manilius — which he had already embarked on at the turn of the century, but to which he consecrated almost all of his reserves of energy in the nearly forty years that remained to him — we remember Housman because he composed some of the most exquisite lines in the whole treasury of English verse:

Loveliest of trees, the cherry now
Is hung with bloom along the bough,
And stands about the woodland ride
Wearing white for Eastertide.

Now, of my threescore years and ten,
Twenty will not come again,
And take from seventy springs a score,
It only leaves me fifty more.

And since to look at things in bloom
Fifty springs are little room,
About the woodlands I will go
To see the cherry hung with snow.

Yet Housman lived remote from the literary world and a recluse from the fame that *A Shropshire Lad* had brought him. His *Last Poems* add little in volume or in content to his first.

The Gospel of God: Father, Son and Holy Spirit, makes me thankful for the beauty of the earth, and for the beauty of such verse as Housman's, and for "the land of lost content" he brings before our eyes.

The Gospel of God makes me thankful for the indomitable courage that marks Housman's long climb from his early failure at Oxford to his final eminence in that branch of knowledge in which the examiners had once found him wanting.

The Gospel of God makes me thankful for the patient precision and near perfection of Housman's scholarship.

The Gospel of God makes me thankful for that voice of deep compassion we hear in Housman's poems, despite his cold carapace.

But, above all, the Gospel of God makes me thankful that verse of such great beauty was distilled from such anguish: a precipitation from some dark and hidden source, and a veritable redemption in and through verse.

But Housman's biographer, George Watson — to whom I am much indebted — was right to call his work *A.E. Housman: A Divided Life* — divided, not least because, for one reason and another, the force of feeling in him was diverted and restricted, but never wholly submerged, by his will and his intellect. Housman sealed off — with an exclusion that came close to asceticism — the sexual and emotional needs that impelled him, no less than others of us, towards the ordinary forms of happiness.

The Gospel of God must surely make most of us feel compassion for Housman: not least because there is some experience in all of us of a divided life; and our heart when it goes out to Housman goes out in part to ourselves.

Housman thought Blake "the most poetical of all poets". I wonder whether in his comfortless rooms in Trinity Housman ever allowed himself to read one poem of Blake's:

A.E. Housman

I went to the Garden of Love
And saw what I never had seen:
A Chapel was built in the midst,
Where I used to play on the green

And the gates of this Chapel were shut,
And 'Thou shalt not' writ over the door;
So I turn'd to the Garden of Love
That so many sweet flowers bore;

And I saw it was filled with graves,
And tomb-stones where flowers should be;
And Priests in black gowns were walking their rounds,
And binding with briars my joys & desires.

I wonder whether Housman, in the sepulchral quiet of Whewell's, and amid the pallid labours of his scholarship, ever turned to that Trinity man, George Herbert, for he, too, understood most marvellously the Gospel of God:

Who would have thought my shrivelled heart
Could have recovered greenness? It was gone
Quite underground, as flowers depart
To feed their mother-root when they have blown;
Where they together
All the hard weather
Dead to the world, keep house unknown.

These are thy wonders, Lord of Power,
Killing and quickening, bringing down to hell
And up to heaven in an hour;
Making a chiming of a passing-bell.
We say amiss,
This or that is.
Thy word is all, if we could spell.

And now in age I bud again,
After so many deaths I live and write;
I once more smell the dew and rain,
And relish versing: O my only Light,
It cannot be
That I am he
On whom thy tempest fell all night.

The Gospel of God is, in the end — thank God! — about One who will gather up the fragments of our divided lives — Housman's and ours — so that nothing, *nothing*, is lost.

131

ALL SORTS TO MAKE A CHURCH

Gray's Inn Chapel: July 13th 1986

"It takes all sorts to make a Church" And the church is "made" as much on Monday as it is on Sunday.

Last Monday I had three different engagements, each of which I think had something to add to my understanding of that phrase: "It takes all sorts to make a Church".

In the morning, I had to interview Leon Murray, who had just finished his year as Vice-President of the Methodist Conference. Leon was born in Jamaica, and grew up on a farm there, one of nine children. His mother was a Hindu, but she sent her children to a Methodist Sunday School. Leon was himself a drop-out from an agricultural College. He came to Britain just twenty-five years ago. The curious thing is that the man who took his ticket at the station at Wellington, Shropshire, when he first arrived, was the same man — thank God — who handed him a hymn-book when he turned up at the local Methodist Church on his first Sunday. Had he gone to a more urban area of the Midlands that would have been much more unlikely.

Leon trained as a part-time Youth Leader and as a Lay Preacher. he was elected to his local church council in 1968; then to the Circuit Quarterly Meeting; to District Synod in 1975, and to Methodist Conference in 1976. After going to technical college he has been working with Guest, Keen and Nettlefolds, who had given him paid leave of absence for his time as Vice-President. His inaugural speech as Vice-President was reported in the papers. After it, Leon received over fifty anonymous filthy letters. But he said he received hundreds of good letters; so he wasn't too upset.

As Vice-President, he has preached up and down the country, as a layman. He told me that when he went to one north London 'White Highlands' church, as he was parking his car a man rushed out and said "You can't park there: it's for members of our congregation" assuming that he couldn't possibly be a member of the congregation! So Leon said with a smile "I hope to be a member of your congregation this morning and to preach to you as Vice-President of the Methodist Conference". Leon has represented the Methodist Church this year in a visit to Sierra Leone, and was particularly proud of the part the churches still play in education in that part of Africa. 90% of the people would have no education there without the Churches.

At the end of last year, Leon was a member of an important ecumenical delegation to South Africa, and was sad to find all the churches divided racially. He found that the majority of white church people he met have no real conception of what is taking place in black townships.

I asked Leon when the Christian faith came alive for him. "Oh", he said "when I listened to an Anglican vicar preaching in our Methodist church in Jamaica". "I see the Church" he said "as the Body which is most capable of bringing people together."

"Yes" I thought, "I go along with that: in spite of our divisions. It takes all sorts to make a Church."

That was with me on Monday afternoon when I attended the installation of the new Dean of Westminster in Westminster Abbey. It was a very splendid occasion, with lots of processions and glorious music. I was glad there were many representatives of other churches, including Cardinal Hume, resplendent in scarlet, from Westminster Cathedral.

The new Dean, Michael Mayne, had started work in South London in 1959 at the same time as I did. We saw a lot of each other. At that time he was Bishop Mervyn Stockwood's chaplain. He has more recently been on the staff of the BBC, then Vicar of Gt. St. Mary's, the University Church in Cambridge. His sermon was memorable; and I want to pass on one or two of his phrases which attracted not only my attention:

Nothing matters more than being caught up out of yourself in wonder.

This must be a listening church: listening to the questions people are actually asking. We must listen to those who differ from us. Nothing is so destructive as doctrinaire certainties.

This must be a questioning church: continually developing in its understanding of the mysteries of God. But it must provide stability and

133

permanence at a time of uncertainty.

Three to four million people come to Westminster Abbey each year. It's a meeting place of the nations: of tourists and pilgrims. And who is to say where one ends and the other begins?.

We must be aware of those who come here anonymously, consciously or unconsciously seeking God.

We must care about quality: giving to people that attention we call love and giving that attention to God which we call worship. We must give the same attention to a wet Monday Evensong as we do to a Royal Wedding.

The new Dean's sermon, I thought, augured well for the future of Westminster Abbey in the years ahead.

I said "It takes all sorts to make a Church". There were quite a number of "sorts" present in Westminster Abbey last Monday.

I went straight from Westminster Abbey to the Reform Club, at the invitation of a representative of the Jewish Board of Deputies, who wanted to discuss what the contribution of British Jews might be to the problems ventilated by *Faith in the City*, the Report of the Archbishop's Commission on Urban Priority Areas. Since March, a group of Jews has been meeting to formulate proposals. They are keen that as a community which has experienced at one time what it has meant to be the less privileged members of the community, and has known what it is to be a minority community in Britain, they should do what they can to strengthen and support other minority communities, especially the West Indians. They feel that their Scriptures, our Old Testament, give them clear directions towards this kind of action.

I found myself particularly moved by this approach. There were some senses in which I could not of course include them within the Church; and they would not want to be included under that heading. But I recollected how happily Jewish members of our community here at Gray's Inn often shared in our worship, and recollected too that prayer in our Prayer Book which begins: "O God of Abraham, God of Isaac, God of Jacob, bless these thy servants, and sow the seed of eternal life in their hearts; that whatsoever in thy holy Word they shall profitably learn, they may in deed fulfil the same. Look, O Lord, mercifully upon them from heaven, and bless them . . ."

And I was thankful that they were in *deed* wanting to fulfil what they had learnt from the Word of God we all share.

Yes; it takes all sorts to make a Church: all sorts and conditions of men — and women. But that last word requires another sermon on another occasion.

DOMINATION ON THE BASIS OF GENDER

Gray's Inn Chapel: November 23rd 1986

"Daughter, thy faith hath made thee whole".

Mark 5 v.34

It has been my invariable experience that members of the Inn treat their Preacher with a generous kindness. However! . . . when I ended my last sermon with the words "It takes all sorts and conditions of men to make a Church . . . *and women*", and added: "But that last word requires another sermon on another occasion", a Bencher greeted me outside with a smile, and with the one word: "Chicken!"

So this morning I shall preach to you on the subject of "Domination on the basis of Gender".

That domination has undoubtedly been the cause of such hurt to some that, alas, one cannot these days bring to the subject humour without real danger of being misunderstood. Otherwise I might have begun what I have to say with James Thurber's marvellously outrageous remark that "A Woman's Place is in the Wrong". But it would be wiser, I'm sure, to start with the Old Testament.

There are very few women who are the subject of Old Testament narratives; notable exceptions are Deborah and Jezebel. For the most part, women appear only in relation to men. Most women appear as a man's wife and as the mother of "his" children.

Lesser categories — the barren woman, the foreign woman, the widow — are categories that relate to what we nowadays call "the main role". The wife and the mother is normally compassionate; subject to suffering, not least to child-birth; often troubled and insecure. Her security within marriage is related closely to bearing

135

children, and if she does not bear them she has not only failed her husband but is considered rejected by God.

Women in the *Old* Testament may make an impact for good and ill, but always within a male world. The context of the Ten Commandments is male. Men are the subjects who are addressed and religious obligations are theirs. The last of the Commandments makes that abundantly clear: "Thou shalt not covet thy neighbour's *wife*."

The ritual laws of Israel defined uncleanness in ways which made it difficult for women to participate in the cult for much of their lives. A woman was virtually unclean for a week after the birth of a son and for two weeks in the case of a daughter!

The most influential Old Testament passage on the subject of women is, of course, the creation story: of Adam and Eve. Eve is created into Adam's world. Women are the source of temptation. "He shall rule over you" is the terse prescriptive conclusion. God himself, not surprisingly, is conceived of entirely in male terms.

The ethos of the Old Testament as far as women are concerned is echoed in the 2nd Century Jewish prayer:

> Blessed be God that he has not made me a Gentile:
> Blessed be God that he has not made me a woman.

Yet I do not believe it is right simply to say that the religion of the Old Testament is responsible for this "domination by gender". The social conventions, customs, and culture in general, happen to be those in which the male dominates. Certainly the religion of the Old Testament does not challenge those conventions; indeed it undoubtedly assists the domination. But any anthropologist would be mistaken, I believe, who threw the whole responsibility for that domination on the religion.

But that only makes the question "Did *Jesus* alter all that?" all the more important. Did the "Jesus Movement" give a new role to women?

One of the most interesting texts in this regard is the strange genealogy of Jesus which is the Prologue to St. Matthew's Gospel. A brilliant New Testament scholar and teacher, Michael Goulder, of the Department of Theology at Birmingham University, has made the point in verse, and, I am glad to say, with no little humour:-

> Exceedingly odd
> Is the means by which God
> Has provided our path to the heavenly shore:
> Of the girls from whose line
> The true light was to shine
> There was one an adultress, one was a whore.

There was Tamar who bore —
What we all should deplore —
A find pair of twins to her father-in-law;
And Rahab the harlot,
Her sins were as scarlet,
As red as the thread which she hung from the door.

Yet alone of her nation
She came to Salvation
And lived to be mother of Boaz, of yore:
And he married Ruth,
A Gentile uncouth
In a manner quite counter to Biblical lore;

And from here there did spring
Blessed David the King,
Who walked on his palace one evening, and saw
The wife of Uriah,
From whom he did sire
A baby that died — oh and princes a score.

And a mother unmarried
It was, too, that carried
God's Son, who was laid in a cradle of straw,
The moral might wait
At the heavenly gate
While the sinners and publicans go in before,
Who have not earned their place,
But received it by grace
And have found them a righteousness not of the Law.

Matthew puts that particular genealogy at the beginning of his Gospel for some reason: clearly for a different reason from the quite different genealogy in Luke. And one thing it is obviously not saying is that God can only make Himself known by a *virgin* birth.

It would take too long in a single sermon to go through all the passages in the Gospels relevant to our subject. But I will state a conclusion with which I think few will disagree: the Kingdom of God in the New Testament is for all — for women as well as men: the woman anointing Jesus in the house of Simon the leper; Elizabeth and Mary; the women at the Cross. The Kingdom is for women as well as for men: for prostitutes (male as well as female) as well as tax gatherers.

Jesus the rebel touches Jairus' daughter, who, if dead — and they thought she was — would have been unclean. To the woman who had been plagued by an issue of blood for twelve years — twelve years of uncleanness — and who had touched Jesus, and who

137

therefore came fearing and trembling — to her, Jesus said: "Daughter, thy faith hath made thee whole".

I will state a second conclusion. Few, reading the Gospels faithfully, can escape the feeling that women are treated in them more positively, at the very least, than in the Old Testament. The welcome which Jesus extended to women, and other disadvantaged classes, meant that they were free to show initiative and leadership in ways that had been denied them within Jewish society, and certainly within Jewish religion.

And then we come to St. Paul! What shall we make of him? What shall we do with him?

I. Corinthians 7: "It is well for a man not to touch a woman. But because of the temptation to immorality, each man should have his own wife and each woman have her own husband." And then, five verses later, Paul makes seemingly smug reference to his own unmarried state: "I wish that all men were even as I". Four chapters later: "I want you to understand that the head of every man is Christ; the head of every woman is her husband; and the head of Christ is God."

Paul, the patriarch, fills out the patriarchal chain of command: God — Christ — man — woman (which of course means God — Christ — Paul — woman). And he goes on: "A man ought not to cover his head, since he is the image of the glory of God, but woman is the glory of man. For man was not made from woman but woman from man." And three more chapters on: "As in all the churches of the saints, the women should keep silence in the churches. For they are not permitted to speak, but should be subordinate, as even the law says. If there is anything they desire to know let them ask their husbands at home. For it is shameful for a woman to speak in church".

Most of us now find such words repugnant. But in so doing we are of course raising not only the question of the role of women but, inescapably, of the authority of the Apostle Paul; and, equally inescapably, of Holy Scripture itself.

Those who wish to find an ideology of "domination on the basis of gender" need look no further than the Old Testament and the First Letter of St. Paul to the Corinthians.

But life in the Church — authority in the Church — and the world — is never simple. As we have said, there is the example of Jesus, and there is St. Paul's Letter to the Galatians:-

For in Christ Jesus you are all sons of God through
faith. For as many of you as were baptised into Christ
have put on Christ.

> There is neither Jew nor Gentile
> neither slave nor free;
> neither male nor female;
> for you are all one in Christ Jesus.

The old distinctions and divisions, Paul is saying here, are irrelevant.

This is, of course, good news and bad news. It is good news to those who have been oppressed, downtrodden and discriminated against: good news to women who have been marginalized and humiliated. It was not such good news to those who had been privileged because of the chance circumstances of their birth. Men, especially men of power, authority and influence, might lose a great deal by being brought within such a community: the community, one might call it, of the *Magnificat*: that song of a woman who magnified the Lord because he had "put down the mighty from their seat" — and most of the mighty were men — and had "exalted the humble and meek".

How different would have been the history of the Christian Church, and its influence on Europe and the rest of the world, if Galatians 3 and the Gospels had been allowed free course.

Alas, the Jesus movement was soon overtaken by much misogyny.

Read the Early Fathers! (But, better not, perhaps, if you're a mother!)

Philo of Alexandria for instance: "The female sex is irrational and akin to bestial passions, fear, sorrow, pleasure and desire from which ensue incurable weaknesses and indescribable diseases". Clement of Alexandria: "Every woman should blush at what she is". Tertullian, John Chrysostom: it is undeniably a terrible record. Augustine: "Sex is degrading to the soul". The pathology and paranoia only intensify in the Middle Ages. Mercifully, time does not allow us to delve deep.

But Catholic as I am in my Anglican loyalties, you will at least understand why I myself have little faith that a whole Vatican Council of unmarried men will ever get right the role of women. Indeed, the fact that men alone arrogate to themselves that right of decision is itself to my mind only one more tragic example of "domination by gender".

I find I need to go back to the Gospels and to the Holy Spirit, in the providence of God, overshadowing the Mother of Our Lord: to the Holy Spirit and that woman without whom there would have been no incarnation, no salvation. The Holy Spirit, John Keble tells us, "fills the Church of God: it fills the sinful world around." And the Holy Spirit, operating through what I will call the contemporary development of our social consciousness, has enabled us to face the unsavoury facts of Church History, and encourages us to go back

139

beyond it to the Gospels, to hear afresh those words of Our Lord: "Daughter, thy faith hath made thee whole".

Alas, so many women have been so wounded by the domination of men that often, understandably, they bring forth a wounded response: not a feminism of wholeness, but a wounded feminism: a kind of theology of the scold — understandably: for hurt breeds hurt. But women are also often evincing a feminist courage which is of the Holy Spirit.

And the wounded Church of wounded men and wounded women needs to go back again to the Gospels and to Galatians 3: which judges, if I may say so, not only the Church.

It judges most professions in England, including, of course, the Law. It judges most acts of worship in the Church of England, and not least ours in this Chapel. For the large and important underlying truth that the Scripture calls us to reflect upon today is that there is not a man, or a woman, or an institution, which does not need in our generation to hear afresh the liberating words of Our Lord Jesus Christ: "Thy faith hath made thee whole."

A CENTENARY SERMON

Gray's Inn Chapel: February 8th 1987

"The Spirit of the Lord is upon me, because he hath anointed me to preach..."

Isaiah 61 v.1. and Luke 4 v.18.

Some of you will know that this is a centenary sermon. I have to congratulate you, or maybe commiserate with you, for suffering, *almost* in silence, a century of sermons from me in this place since 1978.

It is an undoubted privilege to be Preacher to Gray's Inn, and to join the long line of Preachers that stretches back without interruption, certainly to 1574; though I readily confess my inability to maintain the tradition of the first Preacher, who was expelled from Cambridge for declaring in a University Sermon that the episcopal system was introduced by Satan! Neither can I emulate one of his immediate successors, a certain Hannibal Potter, who was ejected from the Presidency of his College, Trinity, Oxford, in 1648, only to be reinstated in 1660. And coming to more recent years, I well know I am not worthy to black the boots of that wise and saintly man Walter Robert Matthews, who was Preacher to Gray's Inn from 1920 to 1932, and with whom I sometimes used to dine after preaching at St. Paul's when he was Dean.

It is, as I've said, an undoubted privilege to be Preacher here; but I will admit that, after nine years, I continue to find the title of Preacher somewhat strange, simply because I have never myself believed that anyone can be a Preacher after the example of Our Lord Himself without first being a pastor; and I have little attraction to being *simply* a Preacher.

It is not without significance that my first and overwhelming emotion today is a sense of bereavement at the absence of those I have ministered to and come to love in these last years here but who are now upon another shore and in a greater light. To name but a few: Roy Wilson, Ray Phillips, Rodney Bax, Brian Gibbens, James Wellwood, Hugh Francis, Muriel Graveson; and I cannot forget the young Murdoch Gair, whose baby I baptised here only days before I buried Murdoch after his untimely death through leukaemia.

"The Spirit of the Lord is upon me", says the prophet Isaiah, ". . . he has sent me to bind up the broken hearted." And I regard that role as literally fundamental to the role of Preacher.

Sometimes people say to me: "Don't you miss a parish?" — with the implication that to be a preacher without a parish is to lack something essential. My invariable answer is: "I *have* a parish: not primarily a territorial parish, but a parish of fifteen hundred of my former undergraduates scattered about the land, and other friends from thirty-five years of ordained ministry; and those associations and the work of pastor and priest at Gray's Inn are the ground of my work as Preacher." The baptisms and marriages here are in fact as important to me as the ministry to the bereaved; and above all it seems to me important, if I accept the title "Preacher", that I should first be able to take on my lips the words of our Lord: "I have called you friends".

When I first undertook the task of Preacher here I knew little or nothing about the Law. It has in fact become clear to me over the years that there is much in common between the role of the Preacher and the role of quite a number of you in your work. In both my profession and yours there is inevitably a contrast between the public and the private self. George Herbert, one of my chief exemplars as pastor, priest and preacher, wrote:

Lord, how can man preach thy eternal word
  He is a brittle crazie glass;
yet in thy temple thou dost him afford
  This glorious and transcendent place
  To be a window, through thy grace.

I imagine that some of you must sometimes feel when you have made some public judgment upon another in the course of your duties the same need of grace that St. Paul knew well when he voiced his concern that when he had preached to others he himself might be a castaway. And I have the feeling often here that we are one with another in our knowledge of our need of grace. You know in your vocation, as I know in mine, that "we have this treasure in earthen vessels". And we know just how earthen those vessels can be, and indeed are.

But if I have need of grace to be a pastor and a priest in order to be a Preacher, it is, I admit, that other role a Preacher is called to fulfil, the role of prophet, that I often find most taxing. Some priests of the Church of England, I believe, take refuge in their role as priest and pastor and refuse the role of prophet. But there is no escape from that role if we are to take upon our lips the words of the prophet Isaiah our Lord Himself took on His:

> The Spirit of the Lord is upon me
> because he hath anointed me to preach the
> Gospel to the poor . . .

> He hath sent me to proclaim deliverance to the captives:
> to set at liberty them that are bruised;
> to preach the Acceptable Year of the Lord.

We have learnt in recent weeks how dangerous it is for any individual even to *seem* to claim to be a prophet of the Lord. Others may call a man a prophet, but it is very dangerous for any man to say of himself: "I am a prophet of the Lord". But it is I believe equally dangerous to ignore the prophetic element in the Gospel.

So I regard it as particularly important that I have been able to bring to my preaching here my experience of, for instance, working with the Archbishop's Commission on Urban Priority Areas. Indeed, I do not think it is a matter of false pride on my part that makes me profoundly and humbly thankful that it was not least as Preacher to Gray's Inn that I penned a letter to *The Times*, in May 1981, making the suggestion that the Archbishop of Canterbury should appoint a Commission on the inner city areas of our land — it was, you may remember, just after the first Bristol and Brixton riots; and in due course, the Archbishop acceded to that request.

But it seemed wholly right last Monday that Lord Scarman should propose in the House of Lords a motion that arose from that Commission and its report *Faith in the City*. It seemed wholly right that a layman, and indeed a Law Lord, should that day speak with the voice of a prophet. The Law and the Prophets should never be sundered. As Moses said: "Would God that all the Lord's people were prophets". I believe a just society has as much need of prophets new inspired within the Law as within the Church.

I cannot forget how shortly after preaching here one Sunday towards the end of last year I took the train to Glasgow and next morning walked along the Clyde. There were forty vacant shipyards. Only one had a ship being built in it, which was due for completion at the end of this March; and there were no more orders on the books. That Monday afternoon I walked around Govan and two or three other housing estates and talked with unemployed shipyard workers. Such people desperately need the assurance that the Law is fundamentally their *friend*, and concerned to bring them Justice.

But prophecy in this global village in which we now live dare not be confined to this land alone. It saddens me that concern with obscenity in England today seems so often to be obsessed with sexual immorality. I know of little on this earth more obscene than, for instance, the Iran-Iraq war, which has caused a million casualties since 1980. When Iraq invaded Iran, most military experts predicted the conflict would be brief, as both sides would run out of armaments within a fortnight. Neither Iran nor Iraq has much military industry of its own. But forty countries have been identified who have supplied arms to the warring parties, many arms producers supplying both sides at the same time. That is what I call obscene. Britain has said that it is "strictly impartial" in the conflict and has therefore refused to allow the supply of *lethal* defence equipment to either side. We may not have sent *lethal* weapons *direct*, but engines, vehicles, landing craft, radar and training, all have played their part in keeping the Iranian and Iraqui war machines going; all have helped to prolong the conflict. And British arms have undoubtedly been reaching Iran and Iraq via sales to other nations, and it is not only our arms salesmen who have turned a conveniently blind eye.

I speak of this subject not because I am "dabbling in politics" but because "the Spirit of the Lord is upon me who has anointed me to preach the Gospel" and the blood of the slain cries aloud.

I hope I have made it clear that I am profoundly thankful to be Preacher here; but there is one other reservation about the role of Preacher — anywhere — that I must voice. In Jesus, "the Word was made *flesh*". So often a Preacher's words remain words. Indeed, for many a preacher it is as though simply to have *said* something is to have achieved something. I am always suspicious that words are wind. You will understand why therefore it is important to me that I combine my work as Preacher to Gray's Inn with my work as Director of the charity *Christian Action*. Indeed, I see the two pieces of work as complementing one another and necessary to one another.

Yet there is a simple definition of the task of Preacher which, daunting as it is, totally satisfies me: it is simply "to bring those to whom the preacher preaches close to His Lord and Master." And that is why on this particular occasion I have chosen the text which Our Lord made his own when he read the scriptures in the synagogue of his own home town, Nazareth. It perfectly sums up the role of the Preacher, which he cannot of course achieve in his own power.

As your Preacher I dare not shrink from taking on my lips the words Our Lord himself took on his:

The Spirit of the Lord is upon me for he hath anointed me
to preach the Gospel to the poor . . .
For as the earth bringeth forth her bud, so the Lord
God will cause righteousness and praise to spring
forth before all the nations.

EASTER AND EDUCATION

Gray's Inn Chapel: May 3rd 1987

"The God of Peace, who brought again from the dead our Lord Jesus,
that great Shepherd of the Sheep"
The Epistle to the Hebrews, chapter 13 v.20.

Easter and Education may at first sight seem separate subjects; but
in the last weeks several things have conspired to connect them in
my mind.

Yesterday I had to preach at the 50th anniversary of the opening
of the school I went to as a boy: Dagenham County High School. I
was one of the first ninety pupils who began at that school as an
eleven year-old, in 1936; and I have reason to be extremely thankful
for its marvellously dedicated staff, although I left school, after three
years, at fourteen, when the Second World War broke out. That
school had a lot to do with my being "raised to life", so to speak; and
certainly I was given by my mentors in those days, in a state school,
an example of "shepherding-the-sheep" after the example of our
Lord himself.

What I did not realise then was that there was only one grammar
school in Dagenham itself to serve a community of over 130,000
people. And it did not occur to me then how much human potential
in that particular area was being wasted, and how many of God's gifts
were left in a kind of educational "valley of dry bones". To change
the metaphor: I did not know how many there were, in those days,
not only in places like Dagenham, who were educationally at a young
age "as sheep not having a shepherd".

It was in fact the revelations of the Evacuation at the beginning of
the War, and the findings of the Army concerning the educational

standard of recruits, which administered a shock to the national conscience and brought to light the Two Nations that still existed a century after Disraeli had first used the phrase. One nation was then half-fed, half-clothed, and less than half-taught, waiting to be raised to life.

There was one Christian layman more than any other to whom undoubtedly the subsequent post-war educational "resurrection" was due: who in the power of the God of peace became a shepherd of the sheep: a Conservative "consensus" politician: "Rab" Butler, who was, of course, chiefly responsible for the 1944 Education Act.

Over Easter I have been reading the recent biography of "Rab" by Anthony Howard. I was particularly glad to do so, for as an erstwhile Chaplain of Trinity I had often to sit next to "Rab" when he was Master, not least when I went back there to preach. He had a fatherly quality about him; certainly he took a fatherly interest in me. I knew well that the two subjects he most liked discussing were India and Education, and I used to enjoy getting him to talk about what he so obviously relished reverting to. But until I read Anthony Howard I had little idea just how much patience, diplomatic skill and unwavering purpose his "shepherding" required to achieve that post-1944 educational resurrection. Nor had I realised just how much was achieved through the close co-operation of "Rab" Butler with another great shepherd-of-the-sheep: Archbishop William Temple. Temple once said "I believe that our Lord is much more interested in raising the school-leaving age to sixteen than in acquiring an agreed religious syllabus". That objective was not finally achieved until as late as 1973.

Those thoughts have been at the back of my mind this Easter when I have watched on television and read in the newspapers the pronouncements of the Secretary of State for Education and of the Teachers' Trades Union leaders.

They have been no less in my mind as I have helped with the production of a report entitled *Of Primary Importance*, which is the work of the Tower Hamlets Primary Teacher Support Project and is shortly to be published by the Urban Studies Centre in Bethnal Green and *Christian Action*.

It has been my privilege in the last three years to work very closely with that project and its leader Geoffrey Court and to see a good deal of some Tower Hamlets Primary Schools. There are 750 primary school teachers in the Borough of Tower Hamlets alone.

What I have been constantly reminding myself is that "resurrection" cannot only be a matter of an historical event 2,000 years ago. It must be a real experience of new life now; in real people now, like school teachers and their pupils; in real institutions, like

Tower Hamlets Primary Schools; in real communities, like Tower Hamlets, Lambeth and Camden.

My experience, not least as a school-boy in Dagenham, has convinced me that teaching should be a specially honoured profession: that within it most certainly is a place for the shepherding of the sheep. It is hard to imagine a greater responsibility than to contribute in partnership with parents to the upbringing of a new generation. Primary School teachers, working as they do with young children, should feel especially privileged as they stand alongside those who are discovering the world for the first time and assist them in their struggle to make sense of their experience. Education is, in any society, one of the main agents of "new life" and of "resurrection".

What I have seen in Tower Hamlets schools has in fact led me to esteem the teachers there highly. But what I have read recently in the Press, and heard on the radio and television, is a blaming of teachers like them, and a kind of teacher-baiting, and treating them as scapegoats, with little real understanding of the pressures upon such teachers. The teaching force is undoubtedly being kicked back and forth between opposing political parties and against a deafening accompaniment of chanted slogans. The talk is often of the importance of 'standards' — and who could deny their importance? But schools in places like Tower Hamlets cannot simply be judged by means of quantitative indicators like the number of examination passes.

I have come to see very clearly that just as "resurrection" cannot only be a matter of history, of 2,000 years ago: so it cannot be something that happens simply in the Church, or even be confined to where a Christian congregation gathers.

I think of Tower Hamlets as a characteristic place where "resurrection" has to take place: a Borough of 137,000 people, nearly 13,000 of them — 9.2% — Bangladeshi: to name only one group of New Commonwealth residents there. But 40% of the schoolchildren are now Bangladeshi, most of them Muslims. Half of the fathers of the children and three-quarters of the mothers only speak English slightly or not at all.

90% of the homeless in Tower Hamlets are Bangladeshi and 80% of those are in bed and breakfast accommodation. 70% of those who are accommodated in council property are over-crowded, let alone those in privately rented accommodation.

It is children living in these conditions, whom the teachers, I think, are shepherding most wonderfully; but, of course, the figures for reading, writing and arithmetic won't begin to reveal the standard and quality of the teachers' care, or the social problems as well as the teaching problems the teachers are bound to have to cope with.

But I've seen wonderful drama in those schools, and music-making; and the schools are above all caring communities, where the teachers care and the children learn to care for one another.

Many teachers in such situations have, of course, left the profession, and the shortage is now critical. Some teachers who stay are desperate to get out, and will do so as soon as they can. But what is marvellous is that in so many teachers, despite all their anger, frustration and seeming lack of support from the country at large, hope and courage seem perpetually to triumph over experience. They hang on until tomorrow, because tomorrow just might be one of the days that produces moments of magic: moments of "resurrection"; and tomorrow they may find they have a political shepherd of the sheep who understands and supports them.

It may seem very strange to preach about teachers on a Sunday after Easter in the Chapel of an Inn of Court; but I suspect that most of you are here because you owe to your teachers what I owe to mine. Most of you will know well how much you depended on the good shepherding you have received; and most of you will know that although it is important that the voice of the teachers themselves shall be heard truthfully in the present situation, it is *our* duty as Christian citizens to pray and work for "resurrection", not only in Tower Hamlets, but wherever otherwise little ones — of whatever colour, race, or creed — may be caused to stumble. The teachers have need of *our* support and shepherding.

The God of peace, who brought again from the dead our Lord Jesus, that great Shepherd of the Sheep, wills that what He has done *for* us all in Jesus He may now do *in* and *through* us: raising us, and the communities of which we are a part, to new life, through the power He has given us to shepherd his sheep.

COMPASSION
Gray's Inn Chapel: July 12th 1987

During the period of the Election, I began to think that the word "compassion" was in danger of losing its meaning. Every politician of every party seemed so eager to capture it. I don't mean the substance of it, of course!

But it would, I think, be a shame, even a tragedy, if "compassion" were to be taken captive by anyone. It's a beautiful word which describes something which is lovely in itself.

When Charles Wesley wrote:

Jesu, thou art all compassion,
　Pure unbounded love thou art;

he knew what he meant, and found just the right words to express it. It wasn't poetic licence or even overblown rhetoric.

But there are several Greek words behind the word that is translated in the Authorised Version of the Bible by the one word "compassion".

When recently we thought of the Good Samaritan "having compassion", that phrase translated the Greek word *splanknizomai*: to love with your spleen, with your bowels of compassion, with a good deal of gut reaction.

In the First Epistle of St. Peter, Chapter 3, verse 8, the word used in the phrase "Having compassion one of another" is a translation of the Greek word *sumpathes*: sympathetic.

There are at least three other Greek words translated by that one word "compassion", and behind most of them are Aramaic and Hebrew words of subtly different significance.

The former Dean of Winchester, E.G. Selwyn, makes a good point when commenting on that verse in the Epistle of St. Peter. He suggests that there is a sense in which compassion changes something of its meaning according to its context. Sometimes it means forgiving; sometimes, being tender-hearted; sometimes it has more affection, more feeling in it, than in other contexts; sometimes it involves action rather than feelings.

That comment has been with me all this week.

When I left here last Sunday I went off via Heathrow to Strasbourg, to talk to Members of the European Parliament and of the Council of Europe about the Report of the Archbishop's Commission on Urban Priority Areas, *Faith in the City*.

In my hand-luggage, I carried a volume of short stories *The Darker Proof* by Adam Mars-Jones, subtitled *Stories from a Crisis*.

The AIDS crisis has considerably changed our world, and if it has so far defeated medical skill and science, it has certainly given new life to a good many moralisers. But there is no doubt that it has also provided untold opportunities for compassion: for a costly compassion.

Some of you will know that people have volunteered to act as companions and helpers and to do everything humanly possible for those who have contracted AIDS, and whose days, humanly speaking, are numbered. Adam Mars-Jones' short stories all come from his experience as one of those volunteers: called simply, if laconically, a "buddy".

I had read some of the stories before I took my seat in the Air France 'plane. What was left of them harrowed me almost all the rest of my journey. There was time left only to read that day's *Observer* review by Jonathan Keates, which I had reserved till I had finished the book.

I have never myself presumed to ask Adam, as the son of a judge of this Inn, *what* he believes; but I could not have agreed more with one paragraph of the review, which states:

> "Throughout the book rings a note of barely subdued defiance, flung not at the god-botherers eagerly anticipating Sodom's downfall or at the dubious yuppie rhetoric of the New Chastity, but in the teeth of death itself; so that although *neither* writer" — some of the stories are by Edmund White — "adopts a specifically Christian standpoint, the work emerges as *potently Christian* in its expectations of our redemptive capacity."

My host at Strasbourg wondered how I was when I stepped from the 'plane. And — thanks to Adam Mars-Jones — so did I!

And I have to say I did not find a *great* deal of *sympathy* — compassion — in some of the very powerful and privileged politicians whom I encountered in the halls of the European Council and Parliament. The problems of the poor and the powerless victims of

European society seemed somewhat beyond their experience and beyond even the sympathy of some.

But on Friday my hosts kindly volunteered to drive me through the forests of the Vosges mountains to the little village of Günsbach, where Albert Schweitzer was brought up, where his father was pastor, and where the young Schweitzer became, at the tender age of nine, the village organist. We visited also the museum nearby at Kaysersberg, where Schweitzer was born. It contains, of course, many memorabilia of Schweitzer's life from 1913, when he was thirty-eight, at the hospital at Lambaréné in the Gabon.

There Schweitzer "had compassion" on the people on *The Edge of the Primeval Forest*, to quote his own phrase. That meant, of course, sacrificing much of the life of a musician, for which he was so superlatively gifted. Dives gave up music in the medical service of Lazarus; and gave up Günsbach, amongst whose meadows and cherry trees I sat on Friday in the sun's declining rays.

Before Schweitzer went out to Africa he wrote great theological works: notably one in which he maintained that Jesus died a broken and disappointed man, because the eschatological and apocalyptic act of God for which he had looked and longed had not occurred.

No scholar of repute these days accepts Schweitzer's theory; but the example of his compassion not only has not faded, but many of the people who for a time despised what they thought of as his outdated and outmoded hospital at Lambaréné now realise that his closeness to the people is something to be emulated by all involved in Development.

Schweitzer wrote frequently on the nature of Compassion, not least in his books on *Christianity and the Religions of the World* and on *Indian Thought and Its Development*, which were published ten and more years after he had gone out to Africa.

In the former book there is this paragraph:

> Indian religion likes to represent itself as the religion of universal sympathy. It talks a good deal about the compassion which we should feel for all creatures. At the same time, however, it preaches the ideal of being absolutely without interest and of ceasing from all activity, and maintains that even the enthusiasm for doing good must be considered as a passion which in the end has to be overcome. From intellectual compassion, the Brahmanist and the Buddhist do not advance to the compassion of deed. Why, indeed, should they render material assistance to a creature in distress? The only help which they can give, without being inconsistent, is to enable the individual to look behind the veil, and to tell him that he must die to life and this world and thus rise to the passionless state.

But there is one passage above all other in Schweitzer which I find not only hauntingly beautiful but awful in its truth:

> "He comes to us" Schweitzer writes "as One unknown: without a name, as of old, by the lakeside, He came to those who knew Him not. He speaks to us the same words: 'Follow thou Me!' and sets us the tasks which He has to fulfil for our time. He commands. And to those who obey Him, whether they be wise or simple, He will reveal Himself in the toils, the conflicts, the sufferings which they will pass through in His fellowship, and, as an ineffable mystery, they shall learn in their own experience Who He is."

If that be true, it is in the act of compassion — perhaps of being a "buddy" to someone with AIDS; it is in the lived life of compassion, that we discover the truth of the Creeds, which are closed to the intellect alone. Perhaps our *true* creed — what we *really* believe — is revealed not in what we say or think, but in what we *do*: indeed, in our compassion.

AN ADVOCATE

Gray's Inn Chapel: July 19th 1987

"We have an Advocate with the Father, Jesus Christ, the Righteous"
1 John 2 v. 1.

Last weekend some of us were privileged to hear Richard Du Cann QC lecture to us on *The Art of Advocacy*. He was so persuasive that this week I purchased his study of that art, published under that title by Penguin Books. Most of you will know it better than I. It is a delight, even to what I must call myself, in this instance, a mere layman.

All the while I read it, I had at the back of my mind that so familiar text from the First Epistle of St. John, which is, of course, one of the Comfortable Words of the Prayer Book Service of Holy Communion: "If any man sin, we have an Advocate with the Father, Jesus Christ, the righteous, and He is the propitiation for our sins."

But when I turned from Richard Du Cann to my biblical commentaries, to do a little preliminary research on the text, I was at first somewhat disappointed.

The word translated "Advocate" in the Authorised Version in that text is in Greek *paracletos*: the word which obviously lies behind our word Paraclete; but there is little or no evidence in pre-Christian literature or in the secular literature of Christian times of the use of the word to mean "lawyer", "attorney" or "advocate" in its legal sense. It has almost invariably a more general meaning: one who appears on another's behalf, a mediator, an intercessor, a helper. And there is little doubt that the Prayer Book "Comfortable Word" should really be translated quite simply: "We have Jesus Christ, the righteous, who intercedes for us."

That is, of course, as a statement, no great decline or diminishment from its more forensic meaning. And it is a marvellous thing to be

154

able to say to someone simply and straightforwardly: "Jesus Christ is my intercessor: He intercedes for me". It is a statement that every Christian needs to dwell on and make his or her own.

But Master Du Cann's book, and its relation to this text, and indeed to my task as Preacher here, would not go away: would not be, so to speak, dismissed by the lexicon.

I found myself reflecting that even Master Du Cann underlines that in England the right of a man to be represented in the courts, and the role of the advocate representing him, has been recognised since at least the year 1200. And I have little doubt that there are books which trace the ancestry of the advocate in other lands and other civilisations further back.

And a thought formed in my mind — parallel to our Lord's words "If ye being evil know how to give good gifts to your children how much more shall your heavenly father give good things to those who ask him" — the thought that, if you in your so-called "secular" life know how to be an advocate, how much more shall your Heavenly Father be an advocate to you, of you, for you.

And the more I thought on what I will call the earthly gifts of an Advocate, as Master Du Cann outlines them, the more they illuminated this text:

"We have an Advocate with the Father".

Master Du Cann has a whole chapter on the duties of an advocate. Some of his quotations are, of course, in the eloquence of another age; but when I read in the chapter entitled "The Essentials of Advocacy" that Quintillian — whose examination and teaching of advocacy, Master Du Cann maintains, is still far and away the finest that has ever been written on the subject — when I read that Quintillian states boldly that "Advocacy is the highest gift of Providence to man", my text was suddenly illuminated beyond measure. If you have this highest of gifts, how much more you may expect to find it in the giver of all gifts. As St. James says: "Every good gift and every perfect gift is from above and cometh down from the Father."

In that same chapter, Master Du Cann quotes Lord Birkett as saying "Without presence there is nothing."

That too made me reflect. Lord Birkett meant of course more than simply "being present": he meant the manner of the advocate's personal appearance and bearing, his authority conveyed to those in the court, and so on.

The effects of Our Lord's "presence", in the days of his flesh in Judaea and Galilee, are often described in the New Testament. It says on one occasion that the people "fell backwards to the ground". The record is so clear as to how the people of his own town reacted to him when he entered their synagogue, and the crowds in Jerusalem, that there can be little argument that 2,000 years ago Jesus was a person of very great "presence".

That was, however, 2,000 years ago.

What of the presence of Him who is our Advocate now? I would like to quote to you a passage from the great English New Testament scholar of this century, Professor C.H. Dodd, who on this very verse in his commentary on the Johannine Epistles declares that the belief in Christ's heavenly intercession and advocacy is no innovation:

> The belief responds to a need deeply felt wherever religion is seriously ethical. When once the conscience of man comes to recognise a moral law conceived as the will of an entirely righteous God, then every advance in our apprehension of the character of God and of his demands upon man deepens the sense of guilt which sets a barrier between God and ourselves. Yet our need to approach God is all the greater because of our sin. How if there be within the Divine Being Itself that which sympathises with us and pleads our cause? The Christian Gospel declares that this is so; and not only so, but that this Everlasting Mercy was incarnate for us in Christ, who as Man had personal acquaintance with our moral conflict and now represents us within the eternal Godhead. If we conceive to ourselves Christ as praying for us (as He prayed for his disciples on earth), then our prayers for forgiveness and release from sin, whether for ourselves or for others, are taken up into His intercession, which is not, as all our prayers are, weakened or hindered by sin (for He is Jesus Christ, the just, or righteous, as our author emphatically adds). That is what is meant by praying 'in the name of Jesus Christ'. Whatever our words, or even our thoughts, may be when we pray (and they are inevitably imperfect at best, and often mistaken), the real content of Christian prayer is that which Christ asks on our behalf, and the Father grants.

But what does that mean for us today?

A couple of years ago I was asked to give an after dinner speech to magistrates. I was stuck for a story, and Master Mars-Jones and Master Edmund-Davies will remember how they came to my rescue with a rattling good story of — let us call him — Caleb Jones, who'd been up before the magistrates in one of the Welsh valleys, conducting his own defence. At the end of the proceedings the Chairman of the Bench informed him they had concluded that there was a very serious charge to answer and that they were committing him to a higher court. "And may I advise you" said the Chairman "to get all the help the Law affords: solicitor, advocate, the lot!" "Never!" exclaimed Caleb "Never! the Lord Jesus Christ is my only Advocate". "None better!" said the Chairman, "None better! But we think you need somebody *local*".

156

It would have been very easy simply to laugh at that story — it is one of the best I now know. But I found myself thinking why that story is not only funny but naggingly serious. And I came to the conclusion it's because Caleb Jones makes two major mistakes. First of all, he doesn't see that God could work through the work of an earthly Advocate, and help him through the skills of such a person. But, secondly, he doesn't see that the work of Christ, the Heavenly Advocate, is what we *all* need — Judge, Jury, Prisoner, Priest.

In my Non-conformist home, in my childhood, I was taught by my mother a hymn which I've never forgotten, and I hope I never shall:

> Eternal Light! Eternal Light!
>   How pure the soul must be,
> When placed within Thy searching light,
> It shrinks not, but, with calm delight,
>   Can live, and look on Thee!
>
> O how shall I, whose native sphere
>   Is dark, whose mind is dim,
> Before the Ineffable appear,
> And, on my naked spirit, bear
>   That uncreated beam.
>
> There is a way for man to rise
>   To that sublime abode:
> An offering, and a sacrifice,
> A Holy Spirit's energies,
>   An Advocate with God.

POWER AND
POWERLESSNESS
Gray's Inn Chapel: November 15th 1987

It was as we gathered here for our Remembrance Sunday Service last Sunday that others were gathering in the small provincial Northern Ireland town of Enniskillen. We all know now what carnage followed. Revulsion was, at first, the only response of which, thank God, most of us were capable.

But, as the days have gone by this week, the sick logic of it all has surfaced. *The Times*, for instance, carried on Thursday a profile of Gerry Adams: elected to Westminster, as Provisional Sinn Fein MP for West Belfast in 1983 and re-elected in 1987. In 1983 he said — and no doubt it contributed to his electoral victory: "It is the duty of Irish men and women to engage in the legitimate armed struggle". In 1985 he said: "The IRA are political soldiers using means to resist armed aggression". But the events of last Sunday made even Gerry Adams extend at least verbal sympathy.

Christians must be realistic. Again and again we need to relate the Gospel to the realities of power and powerlessness at that hour. But how do we do it?

Confronted by the extreme and ruthlessly destructive methods of the terrorist, there seems often only one possible reply: the relentless and uncompromising use of superior force, so that right prevails through might.

But all of us know that almost every situation in which terrorists are involved has a complex and long standing history, and the terror of the state is, of course, often historically antecedent to revolutionary terrorism.

I think, for instance, of my friend Hugh Lewin, one of the bravest young men I know, who wanted to become an Anglican priest in

South Africa like his father, but, after carrying out his conscientious decision to commit sabotage, after prolonged and agonising deliberation, spent seven years in a South African gaol.

We have been learning more this week of the Libya-IRA connection. So often these days what we might call "domestic" terrorism spills over into the international order and disorder. And international power politics and the arms trade, in which few nations have clean hands, also fuels "domestic" terrorism.

And caught up in the midst of this complex web are the blameless and defenceless, like the vast majority of the people of Enniskillen. I think also of the little children I have seen in places like Soweto, with the military and para-military careering around in armed vehicles; and I still remember the children of Eastern Nigeria helplessly caught up in the civil War, the Biafran War, and taking an orphan of that war back to the village where she was born.

Sheer physical power and armed power are very often interlocked with political power: the structure of society in which some are made to feel "in" and others "out". Very rarely can economic power be separated from that political power and force which backs it. Those with power act powerfully to preserve their economic interests.

Whenever and wherever I have been in areas around the world where there are terrorists, I have found myself forced to look beneath the military surface to the question of the "haves" and the "have nots", the unemployed and the poverty stricken, and so on.

It is naïve to relate the Gospel selectively simply to parts of the complex web of power. And part of that web is what we call cultural power: the education, family structure, gender, sexuality, racial and religious attitudes, and so on, which so shape people's lives. The Sikh assassinations in London this week tragically illustrate that.

When I sat down to choose the lessons for our worship today I could have chosen a lesson from the Bible illustrating each of the several aspects of that complex web of power.

There's no difficulty in finding Biblical passages which are records of force met with force: cities, for instance, surrounded till the walls come tumbling down. The difficulty is that God is invariably assumed to be wholly on one side.

It's not difficult to illustrate political power from the Bible, and economic power, and both entwined together when there's, for instance, "corn in Egypt".

There are a number of recent studies of the words "poor" and "rich" in the Bible: several of them, of course, emanating from what we now call the "Liberation" theologians of Central and South America. And the world of the Bible is as culturally determined as the world of any other age and literature.

I suspect that some of you may be feeling that so far I have omitted one of the most important aspects of the complex web of power: spiritual power.

I have *not* forgotten it. But I wanted first to identify the other aspects of the web; for spiritual power is most often exercised in relation to them. Our spirituality is revealed not only, or even primarily, in what we do with our solitariness, but in, for instance, how we relate to the political power we have and to that which others have — and have not: to what we do about economic power, and the lack of it, and the economic power of others and their lack of it; and to our, and their, cultural power. Spirituality is primarily about how we make a responsible use of the gifts God has allowed us to receive, through the accidents of history, in relation to that web of power, and how we use the providences of personal discipleship in our possession of the story of the Gospel and of the traditions of the Church.

I am often, for instance, strengthened by the example of spiritual power that Jesus showed when at the very height of the chief festival in Jerusalem, he chose, with deliberation, to go to the Temple, which was the power house of it all, but also a kind of combination of Scotland Yard and Westminster Abbey, and made a whip of small cords and drove out the money-changers and the animals.

I am equally strengthened by Christ's courage when he sent an unmistakable message to Herod with the words "Go tell that fox . . ."

I am no less strengthened by the example of the Jesus who got up a great while before day to commune with his Father, and to gain that strength he knew he would need for such acts as the Cleansing of the Temple, the denunciation of Herod, the public proclamation of the truth, the comforting of the bereaved and the healing of the sick.

I was privileged to know a woman who was for several years a prisoner in Russia after the Revolution, Julia de Beausobre. In her journal, meditating one day on her torturers, she wrote:

> Is that not the one thing that matters above all? Indiscriminate, all-pervading kindness? Kindness as a mood of approach to everyone . . . except the cads and bullies . . . And why such an exception? Should not kindness be as indiscriminate as the sun? And what about the devilish cruelty . . . It is unpardonable that anyone should be tortured, even you — if *you* merely leave it at that. But, surely, when you overcome the pain inflicted on you by them, you make *their* criminal record less villainous? . . . But when, through weakness, cowardice, lack of balance, lack of serenity, you augment your pain, their crime becomes so much the darker, and it is darkened by you. If you could understand this, your making yourself invulnerable would not be *only* an act of self-preservation, it

would be a kindness to them . . . Look down right into the depths of your heart and tell me — Is it not right for you to be kind to them? Even to *them*? Particularly to them, perhaps? Is it not right that those men who have no kindness within them should get a surplus of it flowing towards them from without? The whole of me responds with a "Yes!" like a thundering throb of music.

Yes; that needs spiritual power; the response of the powerless to the powerful.

I thought of Julia de Beausobre this week when I read of the week's undoubted hero: that father in Enniskillen, Gordon Wilson, whose daughter had just died in his arms, who said "I feel no bitterness against her killers".

But even that wonderful example — in line with and in the power of Him who said "Father, forgive them" — should not so occupy our hearts and minds that it removes from them the reality of our day-to-day responsibility for our part in creating and sustaining, sometimes restoring and sometimes destroying, the world's power structure.

Finally — and I use that word very carefully and precisely, not just as part of a preacher's rhetoric — finally, the Gospel reminds us in our relative positions of power, that the *power-full* of the day of our Lord Jesus Christ: Herod, Pilate, the Chief Priests — his judges — are remembered now only because of the role of their Victim: the man who — finally — could not move a foot or a finger, because, powerless, or so it seemed, he was nailed to a criminal's Cross like a rat to a barn door.

"MONTY"

Gray's Inn Chapel: November 22nd 1987

I have never needed much persuading to take seriously Disraeli's advice: "Read no history: nothing but biography: for that is life, without theory".

As a priest, my attraction to biography has needed no apology; for at the centre of the Christian faith there is, of course, a biography — or, rather, *the* biography which illuminates all others.

My apology — or confession — should be that I can rarely get out of a bookshop without a new biography under my arm. But I don't in fact feel too guilty about that, if "the proper study of Mankind is man" — embracing, of course, woman.

So when, earlier this autumn, I realised that the 17th November would be the centenary of the birth of Field-Marshal Montgomery, I fell heavily. I bought the recent 3-volume Nigel Hamilton Whitbread Prize biography of him, and devoured all 2,700 pages. Even now I feel relatively impenitent about that; for I agree with the *Daily Telegraph*'s comment: "There are grounds for nothing but praise at the totality of the author's achievement, both in the conception and execution of the whole work. It is an extraordinary man, painted as if by a literary Picasso, from many points of view, on the same canvas".

That a soldier like Sir John Hackett should give this biography of "Monty" high praise is readily understandable. But why should *I* find the biography so enthralling? And why should I make it the subject of a sermon?

I should perhaps tell you first that it was Bishop Montgomery, Monty's father, who before he became Bishop of Tasmania was Vicar of St. Mark's Kennington, who in 1885 gave the crucial advice to Trinity College, Cambridge, that the parish of St. George in Camberwell in South London, of which I was privileged to be vicar seventy-five years later, should be the area of the Trinity College Cambridge Mission: which advice Bishop Thorold of Rochester — Camberwell was then in his diocese — received in Torquay, where he was convalescing, as "a bottle of port wine to a weak man". So I had a vested interest. But that would only account for a small proportion of my attraction to the biography.

The early years of Monty's biography are undoubtedly of crucial importance. Bishop Montgomery had met his wife when he was a curate at St. Margaret's, Westminster. His vicar was Canon Farrar, later Dean Farrar of Canterbury, author of *Eric or Little by Little* and of a best-selling *Life of Christ*. Monty's father, when he was thirty-two, had fallen in love with his vicar's daughter, Maud, when she was only fourteen. He had to wait all of two years before he could marry her! By the time she was twenty-five she had borne five of their nine children. Bernard was the fourth and born in the Kennington vicarage, near where I now live.

There's a paragraph on only the fifth page of this great biography — in every sense — which gripped my attention, and held it until the point had been proved beyond dispute many pages on. It says: "Bernard was undoubtedly the black sheep. Whether he would have risen to the heights he did had he not resented and fought against the loveless tyranny (of his mother) one cannot say; but certainly his awkward, cussed and single-minded character was moulded in the struggle of wills between them. Though he came to respect his mother, he never forgave her. Harold, Donald and Una obeyed her in everything; then emigrated. Only Bernard challenged her; and the conflict of their personalities lasted until her death in 1949. He did not even attend her funeral."

One might add at this point that years later, when Montgomery was given the Freedom of Newport, Monmouthshire, and the Council had courteously invited his mother to the ceremony and banquet, Monty, shaking with anger, snapped at the Mayor: "I won't have her here. If she comes, I go!"

There were in fact few signs of the future Field-Marshal in Monty's school days at St. Paul's. He passed out of Sandhurst 36th in order of merit, his lance-corporal's stripe having been removed because of his crucial part in what nowadays we would call a bullying incident. It was in India that his star began to rise. He entered the First World War as an innocent, relatively impecunious young lieutenant. In the first days of the War he was left for dead on the battlefield; but he emerged from the War a decorated leader of men and a staff officer of considerable repute.

In the inter-war years his star continued to rise. The confirmed bachelor, when he was nearly forty, made a proposal of marriage;

but when that was refused, he promptly proposed to and was accepted by the widowed Betty Carver. Next year, his only son David was born; but he was only nine when his mother died of septicaemia after an insect bite. His grief-stricken father buried his grief in his continuing career.

The magnitude and brilliance of Montgomery's achievements in the Second World War — from Dunkirk to Alamein to the Sangro, and from Normandy to the Baltic, are familiar to all. His biographer states: "He was awkward to serve alongside; impossible to serve over, but excellent to serve under".

The biography brings out all the contradictory human qualities of this very strange, as well as very great, man. After his wife's death, Bernard became again awkward, egocentric, sometimes vindictive, often vain. He entrusted his son David to the care of Tom and Phyllis Reynolds, the headmaster of David's preparatory school, at Amesbury, who cared for him like a son. This did not stop Monty eventually severing the relationship with the Reynolds over a triviality.

From North Africa, Montgomery had tried to control his son's life at school and in school holidays to an alarming extent. When, later, David's marriage broke down, Monty blamed his son, and for many years cut him out of his will.

Monty's romantic friendship, indeed, his infatuation, with the twelve year old Lucien Trueb, beginning in 1946 — one of several such relationships — makes it clear that the cold, merciless, pursuer of professional excellence and the emotionally retarded adult moved in tandem. When Tom Reynolds, the son of David Montgomery's guardian, 'phoned the Field-Marshal to tell him of his mother's death, he asked: "Is that Field-Marshal Montgomery?" "No" the Field-Marshal replied, "This is Field-Marshal the Viscount Montgomery of Alamein". Tom said: "It's Tom speaking — Tom Reynolds". "What do you want?" Monty asked. Tom said: "Field-Marshal, I thought you'd like to know, my mother died half an hour ago". "Oh" said the Field-Marshal — and there was a pause: "I'll tell David next time I write to him" — and hung up.

You may say: Well, so far that's a kind of centenary article, on the best British field commander since Wellington, rather underlining his complexity and darker side. But where's the sermon?

Part of me says: Do I really have to spell that out? Isn't it plain for all to see?

First: What I have so far said this morning in no way diminishes my gratitude to the anonymous person who wrote on a wreath that was placed on Monty's grave on the day of his funeral: "In grateful memory of all you did for England". But it reminds me how God gathers up the fragments of our personalities so that nothing is lost — in a way that we ourselves fail to integrate them. Monty's darker side was not a kind of aberration: it was an integral part of the deep raw material of his greatness. It was more like a black seam of coal that may astonish us when we see it suddenly breaking through the surface in an open-cast mine in the middle of grass-land.

The simple fact is that there is none of us without this darker side, and we ignore it at our peril. It behoves us to familiarise ourselves with it, to understand it and be thankful for it; to be humble about its destructive capacities but never to disassociate it from our gifts; and never simply to stamp on it or turn our backs on it.

There's another quite different sermon, I think, in the contrast between Monty at the height of his powers and Monty in retirement. No one would have denied his need of grace when he bore all the terrifying responsibilities of command at, say, Alamein and at Arnhem, in the Ardennes and across the Rhine. But now I possess my own Senior Citizen's Rail Card I begin to see more clearly that there is a special grace required in retirement; which may be an even more testing time to men and women of action: whose action has entirely fulfilled and employed all their gifts, but may perhaps have prevented the self-questioning, introspective reflection that is possible in the more tranquil times of retirement.

There's a third and equally different sermon. Monty was undoubtedly from beginning to end a bully. The lance-corporal who set fire to the shirt tails of a cadet at Sandhurst was also, in the opinion of his brother Brian, a bully to his wife and son. But Providence delivered cards into Montgomery's hands at certain times in his life which fully and positively used all or almost all his delinquent material.

The world, in my experience, is made up of delinquents — like myself — whose occupation somehow gathers up and harnesses all or almost all our delinquency. But many there are whose delinquency is never quite harnessed by their occupation. Perhaps, indeed, they are unemployed, or never find the employment that fits them like a glove. Monty's biography, by which I mean his life, makes me want to pray for and work for those who are less favoured by Providence: whose "hour" never seems to come, though they have obvious gifts. Am I romantic — or even plain wrong — in thinking that our courts often have before them people whose delinquency has never really been harnessed? I can't help wondering what might have happened to Monty — indeed, to Churchill — had there been no Second World War.

And one more sermon. I can never go past Monty's statue in Whitehall, not far from the cenotaph, particularly when I'm the man on top of a Kennington omnibus, without thinking of the man who one morning before he died, in March 1976, said: "I couldn't sleep last night . . . I can't have very long to go now before I've got to meet God — and explain all those men I killed at Alamein".

Monty was always frightened of dying and would never visit a hospital if he could possibly avoid doing so. There's often fear at the heart of men of seeming strength — indeed, violence.

There's a last sermon there about Monty the biblical preacher and teacher, who could speak so easily of "The Lord Mighty in Battle", but whose pedagogic episcopal father and mother failed to impart to him an unshakeable belief and trust in a loving merciful God who would never stop loving Bernard Law Montgomery, and whose love could cast out fear.

Sometimes I think the best intercession we can make for those we love but see no longer is simply "Lord, remember so-and-so when Thou comest into Thy Kingdom", and to make it in entire faith and trust that He will. I found myself making that heartfelt prayer for Monty, born, as I say, in the Vicarage round the corner in Kennington, on November 17th, the hundredth anniversary of his birth, when they were putting up a blue plaque on the Vicarage to mark the occasion.

At the Field-Marshal's funeral, after they had laid his Garter Banner on the altar of St. George's Chapel, Windsor, and after a bugler had sounded the Last Post — and Reveille — the congregation sang as the final hymn the wonderful Easter hymn:

> The Strife is O'er
> The Battle Done

It was a marvellous but dangerous hymn to choose; because, with the Field-Marshal's coffin in front of them, it would be almost impossible not to think simply of Monty's strife and battle over and done; whereas, of course, the hymn refers primarily to that titanic battle on Calvary in which Jesus strove with everything in Him, and strove triumphantly, to reveal as clearly as He could the very nature of the Love of God; into whose hands we can safely entrust Bernard Law Montgomery, and all others we love but see no longer — and ourselves.

WHAT IS TRUTH?

Gray's Inn Chapel: January 31st 1988

"What is truth?": Pilate's notorious question.

I expect that at least some of you had to go back from worship last Sunday and do some work in preparation for Monday.

I went home to try to get through a book called *The Truth — about AIDS* by Dr Patrick Dixon, which I needed to finish before I met with its author on Monday morning at the Trustees' meeting of a Trust to which I belong, which has a very considerable annual income, and which had urgent decisions to take on Monday about what it could, and should, and would do about AIDS.

The question "What *is* truth?" seemed to hover about me all afternoon and evening as I worked my way through the book. Certainly the truth wasn't something simple and single. I've seldom been more conscious of the many-sidedness of truth: not as it sometimes seems when one speaks of the "jewel" of truth; but as something dark, intractable and threatening called "Truth", which is nevertheless many-sided.

There's the truth about the AIDS virus; and, as yet, the *unknown* truth about the vaccine or drug that *may* some day deal with it — please God soon.

There's the truth about the money which is needed for research and who's to find it: Drug Companies? The Government? Foundations?

There's the truth about how people get AIDS; and the truth about what must be done to help them stop getting it.

There's the truth about the nightmare that hits people, one at a time, when they discover they are infected, and hits their friends and families and dependents, one at a time.

There's the truth which religion, and specially the Christian

167

religion, should be relating to this foul and fell disease, and to those who get it — and not just in words.

Then there's the financial truth, to be brought home both to Government and to what we call "the voluntary sector", of the cost of care, in hospitals, hospices and homes.

There's the truth about the state of the Health Service, its capacity, and incapacity, to cope with and care for those who are suffering from AIDS; and the truth about the kind of care which can be given by ordinary members of the community if they are willing to be trained to give help.

And there's the truth — which is certainly not just a series of facts — which can enable someone to live "truly" *with* AIDS, not simply hopelessly but creatively.

It's often some personal knowledge of the truth, or some aspect of it, which heightens your sensitivity to truth. Besides the presence of Dr Patrick Dixon — a member of a terminal care team who has made it his business to master as much as he could of the Truth about AIDS and to communicate it — not far from the front of my mind I had the words of a friend and erstwhile undergraduate of mine, until a few weeks ago Director of Social Services for an inner London Borough: that he was having to make plans for "an emergency situation in two or three years when a thousand people could be dying of AIDS in that area alone, out of 140,000 people". Already, the Radcliffe Infirmary says, about a hundred thousand people in Britain have the Human Immunodeficiency Virus. That has been a sobering insight into the Truth about AIDS.

Our Trust took decisions by Monday evening, made choices, (and decided against other claims) which are likely to involve it in massive expenditure on AIDS; only a fragment, I fear, of what is needed.

But there's one aspect of the truth about AIDS with which we did not need to be concerned on Monday, yet which is a hugely powerful and important aspect of it: the fear it has created, and especially what we now call "Homophobia", which you will well know has done much damage recently within the Church of England, in the form of a kind of witch-hunt of people who are homosexual, particularly of homosexual clergy. Almost every day for the last few weeks I have had a letter or a 'phone call from an unmarried clergyman, working often in inner city areas under great stress, where married clergy and their families sometimes find it difficult to minister, who are victims of this Homophobia, stirred up not least by the media, and who need pastoral support in this painful situation.

I want to say as your priest and Preacher here, that in relation to this subject of homosexual relationships I have myself again been made very conscious of the many-sidedness of truth.

In 1979, the Board for Social Responsibility of the Church of England published the Report of a Working Party with the title *Homosexual Relationships*.

It's a weighty report. The Chairman of the Working Party was the present Bishop of Gloucester, John Yates. It numbered amongst its members the new Dean of King's College, London, Reggie Askew; the present Dean of Durham, Peter Baelz, who was then Professor of Moral and Pastoral Theology in the University of Oxford; Basil Mitchell, the Nolloth Professor of Christian Religion in the University of Oxford; Canon Roy Porter, the Professor of Theology at Exeter, and Professor J.D. McClean, Professor of Law in the University of Sheffield.

All thirteen members of the Working Party came to this *unanimous* conclusion:

> To declare that homosexuals may not in any circumstances give physical expression to their erotic love is unduly to circumscribe the area of responsible choice, to lay on individuals a burden too heavy for some to bear, and, by restricting the options open to them, to hinder their search for an appropriate way of life. In the light of some of the evidence we have received we do not think it possible to deny that there are circumstances in which individuals may justifiably choose to enter into a homosexual relationship with the hope of enjoying a companionship and physical expression of sexual love similar to that which is to be found in marriage.

That unanimous expression of opinion of the Working Party it had appointed did not win the approval of the Board for Social Responsibility which had appointed it: the Report was not endorsed or adopted.

But what can be said, without fear of contradiction, is that the Report of that Working Party makes plain that the Biblical truth on this intractable question is not at all what it seems to be on the surface: the surface of, for instance, the Authorised Version of the Bible. The Biblical truth is very complex.

Then there's the medical and psychological truth, which the Working Party's report makes plain is uncertain and inconclusive.

I have already referred to the Working Party's theological and ethical conclusion, which divided the main Board.

In such a complex situation, and with the threat of AIDS not just in the background, but very much in the foreground, it is hugely tempting simply to cut the Gordian knot: to ignore complexity and differing opinions. In our age, when we are presented with so many problems of such great complexity, it is tempting to resort to various authoritarian answers: to Papal infallibility, for instance, and to Biblical Fundamentalism.

169

But Faith is not something which ignores complexity: it is what enables us to confront it. Fear makes us run away into false simplicities. Faith enables us to live with complexity and to face it.

I have taken as my text today one phrase from St. John's Gospel: Pilate's question "What is Truth?" I might equally have taken another phrase from that Gospel which is very precious to me. Jesus is recorded as saying: "I have yet many things to say unto you but ye cannot bear them *now*. Howbeit when he, the Spirit of truth, is come he will guide you into all truth."

The Spirit of Truth. There is no promise that the Spirit of Truth will give us immediate answers. Indeed, the suggestion is that much truth is too much for many to receive now. But the Spirit of Truth will guide. That is our fundamental faith.

The Spirit, I believe, requires us to be open to truth: open to perceiving it and receiving it from surprising quarters: from those who differ from us as well as from those who agree with us. If Truth is "many-sided" we none of us will have a monopoly of it.

I have spoken this morning of two very serious and very painful subjects; but I have always believed that one of God's greatest gifts to us, especially where the receiving of truth is concerned, is humour. So I end, not with St. John or St. Paul or with some great theologian or ecclesiastic. One of God's greatest ministers of truth I have found is James Thurber, who wrote:

Let us not look back in anger —
nor forward in fear —
but around in awareness.

GONE WITH THE GOAT

Gray's Inn Chapel: February 7th 1988

The story of the scapegoat in Leviticus Chapter 16 is one of the most fascinating in the long history of religion.

To get rid of the sins of the people, Aaron puts both his hands on the head of a goat, chosen by lot; recites over it ritually the sins of the people, and so transfers their sins to the goat. The goat is sent away to "get lost" in the desert; so the people are purged, and their guilt is, so to speak, gone with the goat.

I would be surprised if, when you heard that lesson, all of you felt immediately it was right on the nerve of your everyday experience and spoke directly to your condition.

But a biography has recently been published of the great Trinity College Cambridge social anthropologist, J.G. Frazer, remembered mostly for his mammoth twelve-volume work *The Golden Bough*, first published almost a century ago. In that great work, Frazer cites many examples of scapegoats from all over the world; so that it may not be as remote from our world as we might claim. I am told there are aborigines today in Borneo who annually launch a bark laden with all the sins and misfortunes of the people. They literally "push the boat out". A boat, not a goat, takes away the sins of their world.

The motif of the purifying scapegoat rests on the belief that evil and guilt have an almost material existence which can be moved from one animate or inanimate receptacle to another.

The goat is, of course, an age-old symbol of sin, and particularly of lust.

But however primitive an example of religion the scapegoat may be, it witnesses to an enduring problem and an equally enduring answer: How do we deal with evil? How do we get rid of it? How do we get rid of the guilt that evil brings in its train? "Transfer it",

171

something within us urges; "Project it" is the jargon of the psychiatrist to describe the process.

"Passing the buck", transferring guilt, or trying to, is of course as old as Adam — and Eve; but there's little sign it has no part in contemporary experience.

Even the idea of a personified Devil, with a capital D, is a thinly disguised way of locating evil outside ourselves: of transferring and objectifying it.

A while ago, I visited the vicarage of a friend of mine in the Midlands. It was a small and beautiful Georgian house: one of the few remaining Georgian vicarages. While I was having coffee with the vicar in mid-morning, there was, suddenly, an almighty crash and the sound of splintering glass. The vicar and I rushed into the hall. Half-way up the stairs stood the vicar's frightened seven year-old daughter, surrounded by the glass of the main staircase window. Clutching her dolly to her, she said in a trembling voice, of innocence mingled with guilt: "Daddy, look what dolly's done!" The transference was complete — at least on the surface. It was a sort of "scape-dolly".

It's a hugely powerful capacity that enables us human beings to deflect and transfer guilt, or at least to desire to.

You feel, or you imagine you will feel, innocent yourself if only you can fix the guilt somewhere else.

Vast newspaper sales and profits and the fat fortunes of newspaper proprietors depend not least on the power of the scapegoat.

Fill the front page with the photograph of a psychopath; label it "monster", and the guilt of your readers has at least in part been assuaged. The goat has been sent into the wilderness — to Coventry, or maybe to Wormwood Scrubs.

Much of the blackmailer's power depends on the public's investment in the scapegoat.

Much of the energy that goes into crime reporting; much of the concentration of attention on the punishment of crime, is not what it may seem at first sight, a concern for justice, but scapegoating, barely concealed.

We ourselves become good and pure and virtuous just so long as we can locate and concentrate evil and guilt away from ourselves.

Like Luke's Pharisee in our New Testament Lesson, we thank God that we are "not as other men are".

Fairly trivial sins, like gossiping (which is not always trivial) and scandalmongering, feed, of course, on this capacity for scapegoating.

But major evils also thrive on it.

The more you examine the phenomenon of Jew-baiting: anti-semitism — which reaches back at least a thousand years — the more you find you are into something that relates not only to the Germans of the 30's and 40's but into something that's part of our human psyche, our human nature, everyone's nature.

Whether Kurt Waldheim is guilty or not guilty of the charges that are now being laid against him, the hounding of him is undoubtedly in part the hounding of the scapegoat.

Almost all witch-hunts and heresy hunts are at least in part a kind of 'hunt the scapegoat'. I do not exempt the current witch-hunt of homosexual clergy in the Church of England that has been carried on via the General Synod.

Racism thrives on the scapegoat.

There are, of course, long-established popular phrases which witness to the fact that the scapegoat does not simply belong to primitive and ancient religion: "Give a dog a bad name".

But modern psychology has greatly increased our understanding of what can be called the "scapegoat syndrome". Melanie Klein, for instance, has traced the way in which the inability of an individual to cope with various experiences and their accompanying emotions — anger, jealously, sexuality, dependency, guilt — results in projection onto someone or something outside themselves.

I've already given an example of a child projecting onto a doll. But often a group of children will scapegoat one member of their class at school.

The scapegoat is very much with us in our day to day existence. Many of the casualties of our society, its victims, become its scapegoats: the homeless are written off as "feckless" and left in a wilderness.

To my mind, much Christian atonement theology down the centuries is an invitation to a wrong kind of scapegoating.

I have no doubt that Jesus can and does take my sins away; but there are right and wrong ways of laying our sins on Jesus.

In the end, health — spiritual, physical and psychic health — comes through facing the dark side of ourselves: facing up to our sins and incapacities. Forgiveness has to take place within ourselves, not simply by transferring our sins to some Saviour outside ourselves who in some quasi-arithmetical quasi-juridical way pays "the price of sin". To use Jesus simply as a scapegoat can be as primitive and immature as it was for the Jews to transfer their sins to a goat.

What Jesus does, in his life and triumphant suffering, is to reveal the very nature of the love of the loving God, and therefore his capacity to forgive and accept us and to help us come to terms with and relate his forgiveness to ourselves; in short, to love and accept ourselves. The love he has revealed for us he desires to reveal in us.

And yet that image of the scapegoat is not to be lost and forgotten in the wilderness of anthropology and comparative religion, or even of modern psychology.

It fascinates me that one of the most powerful poems of the poet of our times, Robert Graves, who was the last person to call himself a 'religious' poet, centres on the scapegoat:

Christ of His gentleness
Thirsting and hungering,
Walked in the wilderness;
Soft words of grace He spoke
Unto the desert-folk
That listened wondering.
He heard the bitterns call
From ruined palace-wall,
Answered them brotherly.
He held communion
With the she-pelican
Of lonely piety.
Basilisk, cockatrice,
Flocked to His homilies,
With mail of dread device,
With monstrous barbèd stings.
With eager dragon-eyes;
Great rats on leather wings,
And poor blind broken things,
Foul in their miseries.
And ever with Him went,
Of all His wanderings
Comrade, with ragged coat,
Gaunt ribs — poor innocent —
Bleeding foot, burning throat,
The guileless old scape-goat;
For forty nights and days
Followed in Jesus' ways,
Sure guard behind Him kept,
Tears like a lover wept.

In that poem, Jesus the Victim, the scapegoat — of the Pharisees, of Annas and Caiaphas, of Judas, of the crowd who cried "Crucify!" — is the one whom the scapegoat recognises as a friend in the wilderness, and follows.

And if Jesus is recognised as the friend of the scapegoat, so too must the followers of Jesus be thus recognised in society today: as the friends of the scapegoat.

How would it be if we thought of the Church — and ourselves in the Church — as the Company — the Companions — of the Scapegoat: of all Scapegoats?

HONEST TO GOD

Gray's Inn Chapel: April 17th 1988

"I have chosen the way of truth"   Psalm 119 v. 30.

It has become the habit, of recent years, to centre literary and music festivals around an anniversary. I have been caught up in a not dissimilar event in recent weeks, which has involved me in various seminars, sermons, lectures, broadcasts, and the editing of a book of essays by twenty theologians called *God's Truth*, which was published on the anniversary itself: the twenty-fifth Anniversary of the publication of Bishop John Robinson's *Honest to God*, which, in 1963, sold over a million copies, provoked 4,000 letters, and was translated into seventeen languages.

It's still easier to describe what happened in the 60's — Bernard Levin did it brilliantly in his book *The Pendulum Years* — than to say why it should have happened precisely then.

And it is certainly easier to discuss the subject now, with more light and less heat, not least because it is impossible now to ignore the fact that *Honest to God* was only part of a much larger phenomenon in the life of the Church, and indeed the world. The writing of *Honest to God* and the beginning of the Second Vatican Council, for instance, which occupied the years 1962-5, virtually coincided. "Aggiorn-amento", as it was called then by many, affected almost all the Church, to a greater or lesser degree, and had some significant effects in the world at large.

And now the passage of years has taken the heat off Bishop John Robinson personally, it is possible for a much more objective assessment of him to be made, like Dr. Alistair Kee's *The Roots of Christian Freedom* sub-titled *The Theology of John A. T. Robinson*, which has also been published recently, to mark and to celebrate the anniversary.

Clearly such an anniversary can provide a field-day for religious publishing houses, and a somewhat nostalgic occasion perhaps for those, who like myself, can say, as Commander Campbell used to say on the BBC Brains Trust: "I was there".

But a much more important question is: "What has become of that honesty and concern for the Way of Truth, which rightly or wrongly, was claimed to be at the heart of *Honest to God*?

And I would like to emphasize, as one who was there, that 1963 was not just a field-day for clerics and theologians. One of the most significant facts about that *annus mirabilis*, as Philip Larkin called it in a memorable poem, was that numbers of lay people experienced it as not simply a breath of fresh air but a wind, even a cyclone, of change.

John Robinson was not wrong to quote Wordsworth to describe what it felt like to some:

Bliss was it in that dawn to be alive
But to be young was very heaven.

Curiously, I think I am one of the few people in England who have a particular experience and particular evidence to offer as to what became of *Honest to God* and the movement surrounding it; for in April 1964, a year after the publication of *Honest to God*, after taking much thought and a good deal of advice, I resigned the living of St. George's Camberwell, in order to stump the country in the cause of the renewal and reform of the Church. I had been part of the inner caucus of the church renewal movement, which, mercifully, promised to raise a salary for me, and, as I saw it, consciously and deliberately "chose the way of truth"; truth, that is to say, as I and others, like John Robinson, saw it at the time.

Alas, as I went from place to place, what became immediately obvious to me was how few committed and convinced supporters there were for such a renewal movement: Catholics, Protestants, or what-have-you. The unofficial fortnightly journal of the movement, called *New Christian*, never reached, at its peak, a circulation of more than 11,000. Meetings which I had expected to be meetings of supporters turned out often to be gatherings in which the forces of the opposition, Catholic and Protestant, were strong; but they were not the only opposition: unthinking conservative ecclesiastics, of no fixed abode of churchmanship except the C. of E., especially in the more rural areas, were no less strongly represented.

In fact, those years turned out to be some of the most painful of my ministry. It was all too clear that my friends and I were simply part of an enthusiastic, if voluble, minority. The forces in opposition

177

were large and strong; and clearly a long road lay ahead before that situation would be appreciably altered.

But it was not simply the size and strength of the opposition which became clear to me, but its nature. And in the last twenty-five years my understanding of that may have deepened; it has not fundamentally changed.

What I came to see, twenty-five years ago, was that the opposition to the Way of Truth, as we saw it, was primarily psychological not theological. And I want to explain what I mean by that in the rest of what I have to say to you this morning.

I mean, first of all, that most people, where religion is concerned, cannot or do not face at any depth the question of truth. It is too demanding, not least of time, and too costly. What may look like concern for truth, concern with an intellectual battle between various reputable positions, is usually an illusion; for behind that battle, the real, and more significant battle, goes on: between our security and our insecurity. In that battle, we parade what we assume to be our beliefs and convictions, like children deploying ranks of toy soldiers; but the toy soldiers, labelled this and that, are not the real thing. You have to be very secure indeed really to face, for instance, the complexities of truth; and we individuals are, most of us, so insecure that we prefer to parade our pretended and often unexamined certainties. And the more we are aware, probably unconsciously, that those pretended, unexamined certainties are threatened, the more vigorously we parade them.

Thus ecclesiastical battles, battles between church-goers, about what goes on in church and about church beliefs, are rarely primarily the theological controversies they seem at first sight to be.

In an age of rapid social change, to use the jargon phrase, one must therefore expect an authoritarian Pope to thrive: someone who provides "the answers", the truth, with seeming authority. Alternatively, many will embrace an inerrant or what is claimed to be an inerrant Bible. Either of these will "do" to shield people from the real battle and from the uncertainties. It is the old story of the preacher's note in his margin: "Shout loud: argument weak".

And there are many more ways of escape than two. Indeed, it is difficult to discover something which can *not* be used as a hiding place in the storm on the painful and perilous Way of Truth. People who cling, for instance, to the Book of Common Prayer are often simply taking refuge in a kind of shelter. Of course they will trick out their position with persuasive defences: undeniably the English of the Book of Common Prayer is of incomparable beauty. But that statement does not begin to face up to the intractable question of what should be the pattern of private and public worship in a plural society like ours. But the defence of the Prayer Book provides a marvellous temporary refuge from the real problems of truth in the field of liturgy and worship.

My own conversion experience, so to speak, on this Way of Truth, was not least my encounter in the 60's with the huge number of those violently opposed to what Bishop John Robinson had written, many of whom would have willingly crucified him, given half a chance, but who in fact had never read a word of what he'd written, and had little desire to. The epitome of them for me was the diocesan Bishop, erstwhile Regius Professor of Moral and Pastoral Theology in the University of Oxford, no less, who had allowed his adverse comments to be printed in a Sunday newspaper but who confessed to me in an aside that he'd "never read the book". Perhaps I should add that the failure to read *Honest to God* was not confined to the author's opponents. The 4,000 letters he received make that abundantly clear. Those who were *for Honest to God* were also often clutching at a symbol: at someone in authority who was prepared to probe and question and refuse to accept stock answers.

"What *is* truth?" I found myself asking again and again in those days. And, What is the *Way* of Truth? And I came to the conclusion that psychology and social history could account for much of the journey of many along that way.

These last twenty-five years have confronted humankind with a host of problems, many of them virtually new to our age, which cannot be answered simply by turning to the Bible as a rule-book or to some saviour figure, be he pope or ayatolla: the questions of nuclear warfare and nuclear energy stand out on this anniversary of the Chernobyl disaster; the questions of world population and world hunger, which cannot be separated from the questions of military expenditure; the questions of human fertilisation and embryology. And so on.

At such a time of rapid social change and of so many intractable questions, the majority may well want to evade the way of truth, which demands faith, but does not and cannot deal in certainties — for "now we know in part" — and demands a willingness to recognise and live with the complexities, not least of human nature, including our own.

Authoritarianism in Church and State, will be, and is, very attractive, indeed, seductive. That does not make it the Way of Truth.

There was one question concerning the Way of Truth which I personally have felt bound to face. Why was it that a bishop, John Robinson himself, seemed, the more I got to know him, specially designed, so to speak, for this Way of Truth, and for such a time as this? Why was it he wasn't tarred with the brush of authoritarianism?

Why wasn't he, like others, a victim in the battle of security and insecurity? Or was he? — in some subtle way.

My own conclusion, and I'm glad it concurs with the more recent judgment of Dr. Alistair Kee, is that although, possibly for psychological reasons, John Robinson had need to query nearly every position that could be held, especially every received opinion, every traditional and taken-for-granted position (however radical or conservative) — perhaps because one part of his security, his father, died when he was only ten years old, so that he was deeply aware from his earliest years that "here we have no continuing city", no ultimate security — he had, on the other hand, a massive natural security, from which base he was able to question everything. For having been nurtured in the very heart of the Anglican establishment — born in the Close at Canterbury; educated at Marlborough and at Jesus College and Trinity College Cambridge — paradoxically *because* he was so assured in his security he was able to question it.

In the end, each of us, I believe, by the raw material of our own birth and upbringing, is given a different and special entrance upon, vocation to and calling along the Way of Truth. And it is for each one of us through self-knowledge and knowledge of God's world and of God himself to say our own "I have chosen the way of truth".

I would add only a brief post-script to what I've said. I've said basically that our age of rapid social change, with its huge number of intractable questions, cries out for an authoritarian answer of one sort or another. Our human psychology, in the face of the social facts, is sufficient explanation of why the 60's was such a brief period of freedom — which now, of course, many ridicule, despise and blame; and only want to put the lid on "the wicked 60's", as they see them, and keep it there.

But I would want to say that that wise, saintly and "open" Pope John XXIII — who had spent two years carefully preparing for that Second Vatican Council which began in October 1962 and liberated the Church of Rome, and opened windows that can never now be closed — is not now simply to be written off. "There was a man sent from God whose name was John": John XXIII. And there was another very different man sent from God whose name was John: a very different man indeed: Bishop John Robinson. It is significant that Dr. Alistair Kee decided to call his volume on John Robinson's thought: *The Roots of Christian Freedom*.

In spite of much *talk* of Freedom, in Church and State, there are, I believe, many signs of the Fear of Freedom today, and that we are more and more captive to ayatollas in Church *and* State; and that all of us need to say quite consciously in the 1980's, nearing the 1990's:

I have chosen the way of truth

BAPTISM AND PIERO DELLA FRANCESCA

Gray's Inn Chapel: July 10th 1988

I'm much looking forward to baptising in Chapel here today the infant son of two members of the Inn.

From time to time I like to renew and refresh my own understanding of the sacrament of Baptism. I did it this week by paying one of my periodic visits to the National Gallery, and simply standing once again in front of one of my favourite paintings: the *Baptism of Christ* by Piero della Francesca.

Piero was born in the Umbrian town of San Sepolchro in about the year 1410. He showed an early talent for mathematics, but in due course it was decided that he should be a painter.

To be a painter, in those days, was to be a tradesman or craftsman. Piero was employed at various of the princely courts of central Italy, and at Rome, under the Florentine artist Domenico Veziano; but in about 1460 he lost his sight, and from then on he lived in San Sepolchro, and devoted himself entirely to mathematics and the theory of perspective. These subjects were almost obsessive pre-occupations for him throughout his life, and play an enormously important part in his paintings.

Most probably, Piero painted his *Baptism of Christ* in about 1440, for the Camaldolite Abbey, later the Cathedral, of Borgo San Sepolchro: as part of an altar piece, appropriately for its altar dedicated to St. John the Baptist.

Although the 15th Century was a period of great intellectual advance, it was also one of all but universal illiteracy; and it was one of the artist's chief tasks to tell the story so that it would be easily intelligible and act as a substitute for the written word for those unable to read.

181

"Every picture tells a story". And Piero's *Baptism of Jesus* certainly does. By means of painting, he introduces us to the heights and depths of Christian truth.

Piero's approach to the Biblical account is literal and precise; and the moment he has chosen to portray is sufficiently specific to show that it's clearly St. Luke's Gospel which is in his mind, for St. John the Baptist is in the very act of baptising Jesus: and Jesus is bringing his hands together, on the point of beginning his prayer, while the dove hovers above his head.

Piero has taken enormous pains to represent every detail from the Gospel that is capable of being shown visually, and has included hardly anything that is superfluous to it. Almost every detail has a specific symbolic or narrative part to play.

There's for instance, a figure to the right, in the middle ground, struggling with his shirt as he takes it off, getting ready to be baptised. Clearly Piero means us to set Christ's baptism alongside the baptism of others.

The whole of the left side of the painting is dominated by a huge overhanging tree, which clearly refers to that passage in St. Luke in which John the Baptist says: "Now also the axe is laid unto the root of the tree: every tree therefore which bringeth not forth good fruit is hewn down and cast into the fire." And you can see the stumps of trees that have already been hewn down!

What a warning to those who are taking upon themselves the responsibilities of baptism!

As you look at the painting, you are confronted by the literally central figure of the praying Christ: praying as he stands ready to be baptised. But perhaps even more dominant, and as central as the figure of Christ, is the mysterious, haunting appearance of the dove: hovering, floating above the Christ: the core of both the story and the painting. It's in many ways the most real thing in the picture: unnaturally white and radiant. Of course, it's above the head of Christ, and yet it seems so still, in mid-air, that it seems to lose the kind of earth-bound location that everything else has. It's more apparition than physical reality; the dove descending as a ghost: the Holy Ghost. (It's a tall order to paint the Holy Ghost!)

I've said that Piero paints in order to tell the story for the illiterate; but it would be wrong to say it's simply a simple telling of the story. It's clear that to Piero the truth is never simple.

Look at the face of Christ and you see a seriousness and solemnity that betokens a moment of the utmost importance. It's the Baptism of Christ, and nothing more, the artist seems to say — but adds: and nothing less. His Baptism is Christ's commitment to his vocation: his awful vocation.

Piero's paintings are often said to have an extraordinary quality of stillness about them. Christ praying is still. The dove hovering is, nevertheless, still. The water, pouring from the shell onto Christ's head, is still. It's a moment in time, a very special moment in time, "captured" as we say; but it's also a moment in eternity. Obviously it's not intended to suggest the event lasted for ever; but it does suggest that it's valid for ever.

In the distance in the painting is a town, which has been identified as San Sepolchro itself. Christ's baptism, the painting proclaims, could have taken place there — certainly it says that Christ's Baptism is equally valid in Piero's own day as when it took place, and in his own home town, and thus in ours.

Another important element in the painting is its light. The shadows in part of the painting are what one would expect: the shadows cast under Christ's arm, for instance, show quite clearly that the principal source of light is to the right of the picture. But then you notice that the light is coming directly from above onto the clouds. And the dove, which has a radiance of its own, also has rays of light coming from much higher in the painting. And you realise that Piero, faced with the problem that one of the most important verses in the story could hardly be shown visually at all — "And a voice came from heaven, which said, 'Thou art my beloved Son, in thee I am well pleased'" — has solved the problem by portraying the Father in heaven, out of sight, as the hidden source of light.

I said earlier that Piero was a mathematician, obsessively pre-occupied with perspective. You will not be surprised that the central vertical of the painting passes through the head of the dove and through Christ: through his head and praying hands and the centre of His body. The wings of the dove are horizontal: and the apex of the triangle, the sides of which are formed by the arms of the praying Christ, centres on the head of the dove.

I have not yet mentioned the trinity of figures who stand on the extreme left of the painting. They seem oddly bloodless and pale: more like painted wooden statues than living and breathing human beings. Their actual physical balance is so perfect and so without tension that you can almost see them staying where they are for ever. Equally, there's a remarkable balance between the tones of the colours of the picture. Again, the extraordinary dream-like evenness of intensity, when combined with the physical balance of the figures, produces a kind of slow motion effect and one of "visible silence".

The three angelic figures are usually called the Three Graces: the sisterly likeness between them; the distinctive head-dress of each — the laurel wreath, the rose garland and the jewel — makes it impossible for them to be intended as anything else. Usually, they're shown as a dancing band: in, for instance, the famous Botticelli painting. But here they have a different role: they are totally screened off from the rest of the picture by the tree that comes between them and the main action. In a recent study of the painting, a scholar has shed new light on these three figures: the colour of their robes — red, white and blue — is a clear allusion to the Trinity. The Council of Florence of 1439 had ratified the concord that had been reached between the Western and Eastern Churches, after prolonged theological debates conducted over a period of two years between the theologians of the two churches; and you can even see in the background some Byzantine priests, with their oriental clothes and headgear, looking very much like a delegation of Greek Orthodox theologians today, going on their way. In the clasped hands of the two angelic figures and the hand of one resting on the shoulder of the other, is represented the concord, the important theological conclusions, upon which the Council had agreed: the phrase in the Creed that the Holy Spirit "proceeds from the Father and the Son" — which belief emanated from and was evidenced at the Baptism on the banks of the Jordan and would be declared in the baptisms that took place in San Sepolchro and indeed in the faith of those who bring their children for baptism in our Chapel today. This group of the Three Graces, standing apart from the action, separated from it by the tree, is also a comment on the rest of the painting. In the Three Graces the inter-penetrating love of the Trinity is revealed: "Three in One: and One in Three".

The mathematical nature of Piero's painting itself says something about the very nature of truth as Piero understood it: not least the truth declared and affirmed at Baptism. It will continue to be true that two-and-two-are-four to the end of time. The truths of mathematics to Piero had a kind of "perfection" which made them very much like the truths of theology; so he used the one to portray and symbolise the other.

But he did more. He gave to his whole painting, as I've said, a stillness and spiritual quality which it continues to convey to those who are willing to stand and gaze at it, no matter how many people mill around them, in the National Gallery. Piero has given to his painting what Whittier called "the silence of eternity"; It breaks through even into our busy world today and that moment stills the whole of our world.

So I invite you to take a little "time out". Go to the National Gallery. Take time to be refreshed by Piero's work: refreshed in your own baptism and in the very depths of your spirit.

GREATER LOVE HATH NO MAN

Gray's Inn Chapel: November 11th 1988

"Greater love hath no man than this: that a man lay down his life for his friends". Words from the anthem this morning; and, of course, from the Second Lesson: St. John's Gospel, Chapter 15, verse 13: words which are graven upon thousands of war memorials up and down the land.

Some of my fellow clergy are frankly embarrassed these days by Remembrance Day. It seems to them so inescapably to involve an element of Jingoism. That it can, and often does, there is no doubt. There's usually something of it, for instance, in the Festival of Remembrance broadcast each year from the Royal Albert Hall. But *abusus non tollit usum*. And I find it important, indeed, essential, each year to remember and reflect upon the First World War, which carried off several of my parents' relatives and friends and the Second, which carried off several of mine. And on this day I find myself wanting also to remember, for instance, a young American, Bruce Nickerson, who came to work as a volunteer in my South London parish, one summer in the 60's, under the auspices of Toc H, and who later wrote me an agonized letter, when, under orders, he was dropping napalm on Vietnam; but he was killed before my reply to his letter could possibly have reached him.

Our November memories must surely today also include all who are enfolded within that remarkable prayer of the Pope which I've just used:

". . . the victims of all wars and violence;
  all children who suffer and will suffer
    when people put their faith in weapons of war;
    the multitudes in every country who do not want war . . ."

185

When Wilfred Owen wrote: "My subject is War and the pity of it", as far as I am concerned he was spelling out much of the agenda of Remembrance Day; and Jingoism was about as far from Owen as it could possibly be.

And each year that goes by I find I come across some passage or other that helps me to see the subject of Remembrance as I've never quite seen it before.

It was in fact only ten days ago, when I was reading a volume of essays by R.H. Tawney, long since out of print, that this year I found myself receiving afresh the message of Remembrance Day. "No man alive" declared *The Times* in 1960 "has put more people into his spiritual and intellectual debt than Richard Henry Tawney".

Tawney was, of course, a major figure in the development of English political thought. He was himself a convinced Christian socialist; and some might therefore think it at the least ironic that his writings as a soldier in the First World War should be some of his most moving and compelling.

But what had taken Tawney the Rugbeian, after Oxford, to live at Toynbee Hall, in the East End, and into lecturing up and down the land for the Workers' Educational Association, was the very thing that took him to the Trenches. Tawney enlisted in the Twenty Second Manchester Regiment, declining a Commission. It did not occur to him to doubt that if England had to go to War, and required that so many of the sons of, for instance, Whitechapel, Bethnal Green and Mile End should be enlisted, that he should hesitate to enlist. He not only believed in Equality, but in Liberty and Fraternity; and it was all three that took him to the Trenches.

Like so many, Tawney was not, let us say, an eminently suitable person for battle; but let me read you just one paragraph from his essay "The Attack". It was a fragment of autobiography, published in the *Westminster Gazette* in 1916, which, as I say, I came across only a few days ago:

> When we'd topped a little fold in the ground, we walked into a zone of machine-gun fire. The whole line dropped like one man, some dead and some wounded, the rest taking instinctively to such cover as the ground offered. On my immediate right three men lay in a shell hole. With their heads and feet just showing, they looked like fish in a basket. In crossing no-man's-land we must have lost many more than I realised then . . . Now it was our duty to shoot, and there was an easy target. For the Germans were brave men, as brave as lions. Some of them actually knelt — one, for a moment even stood — on the top of their parapet, to shoot, within not much more than a hundred yards of us. It was insane . . . The worst of it was the confusion; one didn't know how many of us were living or where they were. I crawled along the line to see. A good many men were

laying as they'd dropped . . . We attacked, I think, about 820 strong. A friend told me later in hospital we lost 450 men that day, and that, after being put in again a day or two later, we had fifty-four left.

Sergeant Tawney lay alone in no-man's-land for nearly two days after being wounded by the fragments of a shell. He managed to drag himself back to the Trenches, but was almost given up for dead before being sent back to England.

In an army hospital in Oxford, Bishop Gore went to visit him. The matron hurried to Tawney's bed when the bishop left. "Why ever didn't you tell us you were a gentleman?" she asked.

It was not only that incident but many another in the War that undoubtedly contributed to Tawney's education.

When in 1926, during the General Strike, Hugh Gaitskell was taken by Margaret Cole to meet Tawney in Mecklenburg Square, there he was, sitting, surrounded by an appalling muddle of books, papers and used matches, which his friends knew so well, and wearing his sergeant's jacket. It was that jacket which most impressed Gaitskell: that the greatest social philosopher of his generation should not only have a sergeant's jacket but should actually be wearing it, was, said Gaitskell, "heart-warming".

Before the War, Tawney was an academic — albeit an academic who was willing to come out of the ivory tower of the university; after the War he carried with him a meaning to the words "fraternity" and "fellowship" which he never forgot for the rest of his life. If in 1914 Kitchener's poster — the "great" poster as Margot, Lady Asquith called it — "Your country needs you" — could be placarded on every street corner: if in War your country needed you to lay down your life for your friends: and if so many had laid them down — "Your country needs you", Tawney believed, must be made plain by every aspect of the nation's life: by its employment policy, its education system, its housing, its hospital and health service, its social service, and so on.

The War, and closeness to death, gave Tawney a spiritual depth which he was never to lose. It was evident not so much in ecclesiastical settings — though he was a close friend and adviser of Archbishop William Temple. It was the practical subjects which were Tawney's concern — like education — which he came to regard as fundamentally spiritual. "Education" he wrote, in an article in *The Times Educational Supplement* — significantly, in 1917 — and no less significantly entitled "A National College of All Souls" — "Education" he wrote "is a spiritual activity, much of which is not commercially profitable . . . The prevailing temper of Englishmen is to regard as most important that which is commercially profitable

187

and as of only inferior importance that which is not . . . Education which is given for commercial motives" he continued "will also be withdrawn for commercial motives; it is the nature of the mind to which such motives are of primary importance to take short views even of commercial profit and to grudge the disinterested support of knowledge."

In the War Tawney saw the best and worst of England. Terrible as war was in Tawney's own experience, the immense influence it had on him was not only because of its evil. He was aware that, marshalled against an enemy, war had given to the nation a common outlook, a virtually spiritual unity, an actual power of co-operation and a comradeship in service which eluded it in peace-time. Tawney never solved — and he was not alone in that — why it was — and how — a country could lay down its life for one another in war, but not in peace: why the idea of, for instance, a munitions factory run for personal profit should be so scandalous in war but so readily acceptable in peace. *Esprit de corps* could be the very foundation of efficiency in war — a widely shared social purpose — but not, it seemed, when the war was over. The power on which the country relied for its safety, indeed, its salvation, in war, in an emergency, Tawney believed could and should be called upon in peace; but eventually he was forced to recognise his idealism, and that individual greed and the quest for personal profit might mean saying good-bye to all that. Yet the very idea of a fellowship limited to the business of killing and absent from the business of living haunted him. He was dismayed and appalled that a country which had called upon and called up so many of its citizens could so soon and so seriously neglect so many of them. He summed up where he stood and where he believed all the nation should reckon to be standing: "We stand" he said "upon a world of graves".

Yet it was, as I say, the positive as much as the negative aspects of war which meant so much to Tawney. He mused on the fact that the army, the navy and the air force were called "the services". He had good reason not to be ignorant of the service the services had rendered to the nation, and he knew personally the cost. He was aware that the nation now needed other services — like education — which would also be costly: would also demand that men should lay down their lives for one another; and he wondered why a nation should so willingly pay for its armed services but so reluctantly for its social, educational and health services. Wasted lives in war had given Tawney a passion to prevent wasted lives in peace.

Tawney surveyed the world which had produced the First World War and named it *The Acquisitive Society*. He gave that title to one of his best books, published almost as soon as the signatures to the

Armistice were dry. The Acquisitive Society was one that permitted one nation to plunder another; and to him that was but the concentration of habits that had been encouraged and cultivated in individuals. A society which permitted individuals to take away the dignity of its subjects would end up as a nation which did the same to other nations. It made of society a jungle which honoured power instead of a fellowship which honoured personality. Above Tawney's idea of society was a "banner with a strange device"; for it was really those words of St. John, the truth of which Tawney had been taught not least in the Trenches: "Greater love hath no man than this that a man lay down his life for his friends"; and that to him was the opposite — indeed, the very enemy — of the Acquisitive Society.

But it would be wrong to suggest Tawney learnt only the good in men from the Trenches: that it gave him only a vision of mankind. It showed him also, beyond a peradventure, the ineradicable tendency of human beings to fall into wickedness. That is why *The Acquisitive Society* was such a realist piece of writing. Tawney had been taken to the depths of men's propensity — including his own — to desecrate, to destroy, to plunder, to grab and to kill. It was the best and the worst that Tawney saw in the Trenches. He knew that men were capable of fraternity and fellowship, and of unspeakable cruelty and greed. He knew that England only deserved to win the War, and that its people were only worthy of those of his comrades who had sacrificed their lives, if fellowship replaced acquisitiveness as the rationale of the social order.

I have been speaking almost entirely of the First World War; but I doubt whether it will have altogether escaped any of you that I have also been making at least oblique reference to the here and now. It was in fact on my way up to Kirkby, that huge estate a dozen miles outside Liverpool, where 40,000 people are housed, that I read in the train, ten days ago, Tawney's essay. I had asked to be furnished in Kirkby with certain facts and figures — for instance, the facts about the employment of those who left school this last summer. I was told that at the present on average only six out of a hundred have a job since they left school; and I thought of that phrase "Your country needs you"; and I *wondered*. I know that if another war came — which God forbid — they would be needed then.

When Tawney wrote of the time when as Sergeant Tawney he led his men out into the Battle of the Somme, he said: "People and societies walk between precipices, and they do not know the rottenness in them until they crack". He recalled at that time some lines from *The Pilgrim's Progress* which had always struck him, he said, as one of the most awful things imagined by man: "Then I saw that there was a way to Hell, even from the Gates of *Heaven*, as well

189

as from the City of Destruction". "To have gone so far", he wrote, "and to have failed at the last!"

I believe I should be failing in my duty this Remembrance Day — as a patriot and as your Preacher — if I did not declare to you my own conviction that our society is walking between precipices today, and there is no little evidence of what Tawney had in mind when he spoke of its "rottenness", because we are spurning the way of that "Greater Love": of "laying down our lives" for one another and choosing again the seeming secular heaven of the Acquisitive Society. Mercifully, there is not only a way to Hell from the Gates of that sort of Heaven but a way to the true Heaven — the Kingdom of Heaven — from the very Gates of Hell. Please God we shall as individuals and as a nation yet choose that way.

WHEN THOU SHALT BE OLD

Gray's Inn Chapel: November 20th 1988

"When thou wast young, thou girdest thyself, and walkedst whither thou
wouldest; but when thou shalt be old, thou shalt stretch forth thy hands,
and another shall gird thee, and carry thee whither thou wouldest not."

John 21 v.18.

I want to preach to you a memorial sermon this morning to
someone whom most of you will never have met; but I'd like to share
with you what she meant to me; and in fact I think her life has a good
deal to say to us all.

I first knew Janet Lacey — later CBE., and DD. (Lambeth) —
when I was a boy, in Dagenham; but I saw a good deal of her in her
middle years when she was Director of Christian Aid, and in her
declining years. I knew her, that's to say, in her days of darkness as
well as of light, indeed of limelight.

Janet had a Sunderland childhood and adolescence, and if you met
her in her later years you always heard echoes of Sunderland in her
voice. She told the story of her childhood briefly in a book: *A Cup
of Cold Water*. Let's just say: it wasn't a childhood calculated to
produce a smooth adult.

Her first promising years out at work were with the YWCA in
Kendal. They were "promising" because of her unique mix of gifts:
of drama, music, community work and theology, which were already
apparent, then and there.

But as I've said, I got to know Janet personally through the
remarkable work she did next, in Dagenham: at the joint
YMCA/YWCA community centre at the heart of the huge housing
estate of 130,000, just before and during the Second World War.
Within weeks of her dying, her friend Sidney Russell, Warden of the

191

settlement, Kingsley Hall, in Dagenham, also died. Somewhere up in Heaven's sublimest glory those two will now be telling God about Dagenham; and while that's going on there certainly won't be silence in heaven!

It was in those Dagenham days that people first saw Janet's full possibilities. She could be as tough as old boots but very tender too; and it was the combination of the two which made people realise what she had it in her to give later, in, for instance, the hideously demanding situation of immediately post-war Germany.

It was typical of Janet that when she was supposed to be dealing with soldiers — with the education of British soldiers, via the YMCA — she contrived to do as much for German young people; and that work she managed to continue when she became Secretary of the Youth Department of the British Council of Churches. She was deeply shocked while with the BAOR in Germany at the devastation of the towns and cities. One morning she reached her office and realised with shame that she had walked through the ruined streets without noticing. "I sat down and vowed to myself then and there" she recalled later, "that never, never again, would I allow myself to get used to human suffering." And in all her subsequent visits to refugee camps, Third World slums and areas of oppression, like South Africa, she never did.

Twenty-one years with the British Council of Churches must constitute a virtually unique as well as most remarkable record of service.

I was still relatively young — twenty-six and just ordained — when I was able to witness and admire the flair she evinced in, for instance, her contribution to the first British Conference of Church Youth at Bangor in 1951. She was then about to undertake what was undoubtedly her greatest work: her pioneer work with the Department of Inter-Church Aid and Refugee Service, which she raised up from the very earth to be at least the shape of things to come of Christian Aid as we know it now, complete with Christian Aid Week. She raised the annual income of Christian Aid from next to nothing to two million pounds.

But besides her contribution to the British Council of Churches through Inter-Church Aid, there was what she gave to the World Council of Churches: not least the memorable play-cum-pageant *By the Waters of Babylon*, which she herself wrote and produced for the Second Assembly at Evanston, Illinois, in 1954. What Janet achieved at Evanston meant that she had more than a finger in the drama and film side of the Third Assembly of the World Council of Churches at New Delhi in 1960 and the Fourth Assembly at Uppsala in 1968.

In January 1972, when I was visiting Uganda — in the first year of Amin's regime, when the scale of the tragedy that lay ahead was not yet fully apparent — I went one afternoon to the Kitwe Community Centre, in the heart of the worst slums of Kampala.

I'd rarely been so impressed with a centre. Thee was a primary school, a clinic, adult education, youth work, trades teaching, community development, and so on. It was financed jointly by the Uganda Christian Council, Oxfam and Christian Aid.

As I walked through the crowded and busy buildings, I caught sight of the foundation stone, with its engraved lettering: "This foundation stone was laid by Janet Lacey, Director of Christian Aid", and the day, the month and the year: 1963. Of course I was not surprised; but I remember my heart suddenly missed a beat at seeing Janet's name, and then gave a kind of lift of affection and of proud thanksgiving.

That fairly typical situation in Uganda could well stand for all Janet's contribution to Christian Aid, though it was a varied and manifold work.

And the time would fail me to tell of Janet's part in the beginnings of VSO; of her work with the Family Welfare Association and with the Churches Council for Health and Healing: work which is still bearing fruit at Marylebone Parish Church today.

But I'm not going to list Janet's life like an obituary, even though, as I've said, I wanted to memorialize her here today. I would rather reflect on something of what I can only call the mystery of it all.

"When thou wast young, thou girdest thyself, and walkedst whither thou wouldest". Yes; that Janet did — except that Janet rarely walked anywhere. Janet went by taxi — and flew — to the ends of the earth. Although her work took her amongst the poorest of the poor, when she got back to England she treated herself to taxis and rather up-market meals.

There was about Janet in those earlier years a refreshing freedom, a dominance, a creative vigour, which was a wonder to many of us — though sometimes it could border on violence — and did — when she could be very intimidating. But in such a human being it was difficult to see how we could have had the blessings of that strength without sometimes the curses. I've come to the conclusion that God sanctifies bull-dozers for the cause of his Kingdom as well as "little flowers". With Janet, you quickly came to expect contradictions: realism and shrewdness one moment, blind fantasy the next; massive strength, energy, efficiency and competence, coupled with surprising incapacities; compassion and care for the individual — and, at times, elephantine insensitivity. Janet had the faults and virtues of greatness.

Some of us, for instance, whom she would take to the theatre or to a restaurant — or back to her flat to admire the latest work of art she had added to her collection: a new Arthur Dooley, or something in copper from Zambia or in batik from Bandung — some of us began to wonder what would happen to Janet when she was old.

We wondered, not least, because there were always odd things about her: you were never allowed to take *her* to a theatre — or pay your own way at a restaurant; and in those days it was not equal pay and pensions for women; and you began to wonder how it would all end. Those visits to the theatre and those meals were marvellous. It was alright while she was young enough and strong enough to "gird herself"; but what would happen when she was old?

I shan't forget how, suddenly, Janet allowed me to talk over with her all that.

By chance she had seen me doing something on Television one evening, and must have resolved there and then to talk. She 'phoned, and I knew I must go to her immediately. I remember it was as though all that mountainous strength had suddenly collapsed. She knew she couldn't cope: could no longer 'gird herself'. She who had saved others knew that herself she could not save. It was, of course, a moment of depression — which later one had virtually to pretend had never occurred. (We all need — have a right to — our pretences as defences, and no one should presume to rip them away: certainly not when confidences have been shared.) It was a moment of depression, but it was also a moment of truth that revealed more than the truth of that moment. "Eric" she said "I just can't live within my means. And I daren't move because no one will come to see me". (She lived between Victoria Station and Westminster Abbey.)

And then came the very last sad years. "When thou shalt be old, thou shalt stretch forth thy hands, and another shall gird thee, and carry thee whither thou wouldest not." Janet's last years, with the grim disintegration of Alzheimer's disease, until her death this year at eighty-five, were particularly distressing — in view of her first years: not that her ox-like energy entirely vanished. She did not "go gentle into that good night". Sometimes — thank God! — she raged "against the dying of the light" in the home in Kensington where she was "in care".

The mystery of Janet's old age is, in a sense, all of a piece in some way with the mystery of her youth and of her middle years. All that constellation of gifts in the first part of her life is a marvellous mystery, and so is their sudden decline; and both have something to say to us all, particularly to those of us who now form that one in five of the population that is over sixty. We have all had our gifts, but we lose them in differently mysterious ways. If anyone can provide me with a theology of Alzheimer's disease, I should be very grateful. I haven't one myself. All I can do is to take on my lips those words of our Lord on the Cross: "My God, My God, WHY?"

Perhaps I should insert here that Janet — like me — was brought up as a Methodist. But she was confirmed in the height of her years with Christian Aid. I think it was the mystery of worship that she had discovered, having been brought up primarily on preaching. (By the way: she was the first women to preach in St. Paul's Cathedral and she preached very well.) But, as I say, she discovered mystery at the heart of things, and wanted forms of worship in which she could lose herself in the mystery.

I'm glad to say that it was from a noted "ecumaniac" — Hans Rudi Weber, Director for Biblical Studies at the WCC since 1971, that I received some light on the mystery of Janet's sufferings — from his book *On a Friday Noon: Meditations Under the Cross*: a book that is full of just the kind of illustrations which Janet so loved — from East Africa, Peru and so on. Opposite a 1960 painting of the Crucifixion by a North American artist, William Congdon, there is this passage from that courageous American Jesuit, Daniel Berrigan:

> Suffering often takes the most personally humiliating and opaque character. It incapacitates a man from the very good which was the cause of his greatness in the first place. He can no longer act with that spontaneity and clarity which had so won others. He is now thrown upon the mercy of others, a burden to them; more, he is bewildered and unable to give an account of himself. He cannot explain why or how he suffers; even though once he could reveal, winningly and joyfully, why life took the shape it did, why it was right and fitting that it did so. The scandal of such suffering, suffering that plucks the tongue from the head and the voice from the heart! even to the point that others are scandalized and bewildered. They had concluded over the years that, whatever came to pass, this man would never cease to be their oracle; the years would only confer on him a clearer, more communicable wisdom. But to be reduced to this?

> *Cui bono?* Man does not suffer that a world may be one; he does not suffer, even, that the will of God may be accomplished. He is, in fact, in the deepest suffering, evacuated of all real purpose at all. He is not suffering 'in order that'. His anguish does not allow him to be carried beyond the fact of suffering. And this is true so that the truth of suffering, its value as sign, may shine forth. But only for the few who are ready to read such a sign.

> Achievements, great moments, visible accomplishments, always have about them so much danger of distraction, egoism, ambiguity. But the sufferer who believes and takes his stand, not precisely on his suffering, nor on the quality of his faith, nor on the 'good' he is doing, nor on the

response of his friends, but on Christ alone; which is to say, on the living truth of things — this man, perhaps for the first time, has become a true sign. He is the sign of the cross. There is quite possibly no other in the world today.

Well, we could many of us gladly and thankfully receive the sign that Janet was, in, for instance, her Christian Aid years: the years of her "visible achievement". Could we receive the sign that she was in those last helpless Kensington nursing home years?

There are a very great many people now in homes for the elderly, like the one Janet was in, and in psycho-geriatric wards. Alas, there are also many on our streets — thanks to our present policies — who should be in psycho-geriatric wards, but they are now closed: many whose suffering is apparently evacuated of all real purpose at all.

It is our Christian faith that the darkness did not and does not ever eclipse, overwhelm, comprehend the light — in spite of all appearances. "If I go down to hell, thou art there also."

Janet, even in her strongest days, knew well, in her deep heart's core, that her strength was real, but was also a real facade, and that her weakness was as real as her strength. The mystery of her weakness did not begin when her strength gave out.

Here today I want publicly to be thankful for Janet Lacey's strength and weakness. In God's use of her in strength and weakness we have a sign of what God wills to do with us all — has done with us all — is doing with us all; and all this surely turns our hearts again to the Christ whose Cross that Friday at Noon is the very sign of the weakness and of the strength of God, and of his strength which is made perfect in weakness.

"When thou wast young, thou girdest thyself, and walkedst whither thou wouldest; but when thou shalt be old, thou shalt stretch forth thy hands, and another shall gird thee, and carry thee whither thou wouldest not." That text surely has something to say not only about Janet but about us all, and about the love of God which remains behind the mystery of the darkness of our lives as well as the light.